Spiritual Symbols with Their Meaning

by Nataša Pantović

A⭑L Mindfulness Book #8

Art ⭑ eLements

Published by: Artof4Elements

The Art of 4 Elements

○ △ □ ◎

www.artof4elements.com

Printed 2018

DEDICATION

To all Mindfulness and Alchemy Explorers who see the beauty in every-day Nature & Universal sacred language of symbols and signs. We will not talk about spiritual symbols worshiped by major religions but about trees, numbers, spirals that we meet daily.

Through symbols to mindfulness meditations.

Contents

INTRODUCTON

Symbols and signs are the languages of the soul. Symbols and signs are the language of dreams. Occultists believe that signs and symbols are given a supernatural power at their creation. Words, signs and symbols, images, colors, light, are all used for eons to convey a spiritual meaning.

The Mystics, the Magi initiates, the guardians of the oracle mysteries acquired deep knowledge of the laws of the spiritual world and their interaction with the sense world. Some of them worked hard all through their lives to decipher the spiritual forces behind the forces of nature and to learn how to control the elements.

The Mystics of India

In ancient India the philosophers and the yogis observed the world as an illusion. Yet, the magic of the spiritual world stayed deeply connected to the sense world. Within the science of yoga, the science of mind, body and soul is beautifully correlated. The way we breathe influences the world around us, our perception of the worldly phenomena, our happiness. The way we treat our spine influences our health and wellbeing. Finally the way we treat our thoughts, or the science of mindfulness and meditation influences our current incarnation and the incarnations to come.

Patanjali, within his Yoga Sutras, gives a foundation of the science of Yoga, or the 'Kingly Science of the Soul', mapping the step by step rules, and methods, to make a man perfect, leading him or her from an average person, through to initiates, to a master yogi. A yogi aims to free him / herself from the moods, longings, desires, and emotional reactions that are ruling the life of an average person and has arrived at the point of peace.

The Mystics of Greece

For the philosophers of ancient Babylonia and Greece the sense world was not considered an illusion.

In the search for Divine, they turned towards art, towards symbols and signs within myths and legends. They created such a marvel of art that every detail became an expression of the spiritual. In mysterious ways the wisdom of the initiates poured into poets, artists, and thinkers. They awakened powers of thought and feeling that are not directly stimulated by the spiritual world. Manipulating the elements, they turned towards the Lady Science and carried her principles to the point that we are now able to manipulate the sound, the light, the matter and its manifestation.

The Mystics of China

Chinese created I Ching that within its symbolism reflects the universe in miniature. The book is at the heart of Confucian thought and Taoism, but also a common tool amongst the fortune tellers that use it as a divination text and a roadside oracle. Longmei Zi, early 13th century, depicts Qian and Kun.

The I Ching starts with the hexagrams Qian and Kun. Qian is heaven and Kun is earth. Qian (☰) and Kun (☷), the male and female principles.

When heaven and earth are born, the whole of creation comes into being. All the lines of Qian are masculine, its symbol is the dragon. Kun is earth. It is purely feminine. Earth creates the world and the whole of creation counts on it for nurture and growth. Kun is the female horse.

The Mystics of Kabbalah

Kabbalists designed the Tree of Life and the Tarot symbolism followed it. Kabbalah is an esoteric teaching, a science that explores metaphysical principles of the universe. Any material object and action from both the micro and the macro world is controlled by the spiritual forces.

Kabbalah attempts to understand these spiritual sources, to know their nature and properties. Within the basic structure of the Tree of Life we find the ten Sefirots, each corresponding to a divine quality. They divide into masculine and feminine qualities. The Sefirots are a blue-print of all the phenomena from cosmic forces to human relationships. The Sefirots are linked together in precise relationships and governed by the three divine principles: balance - Will, expansion – Mercy, and constraint - Justice.

The Tarot is used as a symbolic reflection of the Tree of Life, a remarkable repository of esoteric knowledge and a powerful tool for spiritual and psychological exploration.

Mystics Magic and God

To a Chinese sage, a Yogi, and a Cabbalist Mystic, the earth is a field of activity that has to be transformed, so that it carries an imprint of human will.

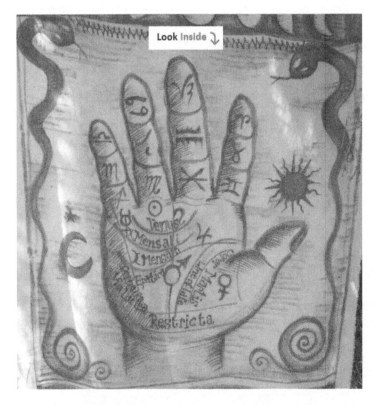

Just as God is hidden, so are the inner secrets of Her divine message. We read about them, hear them uttered, but we cannot possibly comprehend their meaning unless we have a direct experience of their truth. That is why to be able to talk to our souls we use meditation, we use rituals, symbols and signs, we use dreams and careful observation of souls' subconscious messages. The mystics of our past help us in this quest. From Zarathustra who comes from the ancient Persian spiritual culture, to Pythagoras who comes from the Greco-Latin cultural epoch, to Lao Tzu, Buddha and Christ, they all carry the keys to the secrets of the most varied mysteries.

Pythagoras (600 BC) had a simple and elegant manner of explaining his theory of cosmos, God, trinity. He draw a figure, Tetractys that as an esoteric symbol, remained a vital model of the Pythagorean Schools, Pythagoreanism, becoming an expression of their system of metaphysical ideals. The one point was a symbol of the omnipotent Creator, the two points, a female number, of the Female Principle or Matter, the three of the world proceeding from their union, creating the four of the four elements, completing the image of the manifestation.

Hermes Four Elements Symbols Alchemy

Babylon Symbols

Kesh Temple hymn is an Old Babylonian Tablet at the British Museum from 2400 BC, is our first ever published book.

Scholars have disagreed when written records become literature, yet the earliest literary authors known by name are Ptahhotep (who wrote in Egyptian) and Enheduanna (who wrote in Sumerian), dating to around 2400 BC.

Priestess Enheduanna is the earliest known poet whose name has been recorded. She was the High Priestess of the goddess Inanna and the moon god Nanna (SiN). She lived in the Sumerian city state of Ur in Syria. During the 3,000 BC, an intimate cultural symbiosis developed between the Sumerians and Akkadians so the scholars believe that this was the bilingual environment.

Inanna is an ancient Mesopotamian Goddess

Inanna is an ancient Mesopotamian goddess associated with love, beauty, sex, fertility, justice, a bit like Venus. Originally worshipped in Sumer was later worshipped by the Akkadians, Babylonians, and Assyrians under the name iSHtar. She was known as the "Queen of Heaven" and her symbols were the lion and the eight-pointed star. Her husband was the god Dumuzid and her suKKal, or personal attendant, was the goddess NinSHubur.

Eight Pointed Star in Gold

SiN or MooN Godess and Sumerian Temple Hymns

Sīn or Suen (Akkadian: EN.ZU or lord-ess of wisdom) or Nanna was the number 30, in cuneiform 10 x 3 the goddess of the moon in the Mesopotamian religions of Sumer, Akkad, Assyria and Babylonia. Nanna (the classical Sumerian spelling is DŠEŠ.KI = the technical term for the crescent moon, also refers to the deity, is a Sumerian deity worshiped in Ur (Syria you must have guessed).

Enheduanna's contributions to Sumerian literature, include the collection of hymns known as the "Sumerian Temple Hymns", 37 tablets to be exact, from 2,700 BC. The temple hymns were the first collection of their kind, the copying of the hymns indicates that they were used long after and held in very high esteem. Her other famous work is 'The Exaltation of Inanna' or 'Nin-Me-Sar-Ra' which details Enheduanna's expulsion from Ur.

With the tendency to centralize the powers of the universe, the "wisdom" personified by the moon god, has established the own triad of Sin/EN.ZU, his wife and children, 2 kids: Sun and Inanna/Ishtar (Venus). EN.ZU had a beard made of lapis lazuli and rode on a winged bull. The bull was one of his symbols, along with the crescent and the tripod.

Nanna's chief sanctuary at Ur was named E-gish-shir-gal, "house of the great light". It was at Ur that the role of the Priestess was established, as a powerful role held by the princess Enheduanna, and the primary cult role associated with Nanna/Sin.

SiN also had a sanctuary at the city of HaRRan, named E-hul-hul, "Place of singing to H". The cult of the moon-god spread to other centres, so that temples are found in all the large cities of Babylonia and Assyria. A sanctuary for Sin with Syrian inscriptions invoking his name dating to 200 AC was found in the Tektek Mountains, not far from all the legendary Moses (Mo-She) and his burning bush stories of our so much cited and loved Old Testament.

The Kesh Temple Liturgy

The Sumerian Temple Hymns are also known as the Kesh Temple Liturgy to Nintud on the creation of man and woman. Held in the Ashmolean in Oxford, UK in 1913, in "Babylonian Liturgies", the prism contains around 145 lines in eight sections, Langdon called it "A Liturgy to Nintud, Goddess of Creation" and noted that each section ended with the same refrain, which he interpreted as referring:

"to the creation of man and woman, the Biblical Adam and Eve."

The translations speak of the temple reaching both for the heaven and descending into the underworld. The gods and functions of the temple are described: its interior and exterior appearance, its gate, courtyard, door and walls. The hymn discusses music played at the temple with drums and the sound of a bull's horn played at temple ceremonies. The hymn finishes with a "word" repeated four times as an invocation of the divine presence in the temple. The Mystery of Babylon Tower

Other translations were made from tablets in the Nippur collection of the Museum of the Ancient Orient in Istanbul. A further tablet source of the myth is held by the Louvre in Paris.

The lovers of LOVE will rejoice hearing that Babylon founder were indeed called Amorites... The Amorites led a revolution of their times (2,000 BC North Africa), they freed citizens from taxes, distributed Church land to citizens, abolished forced labor, spread education building most amazing cities and their priestesses have written the first ever books worshipping Goddess Moon...

Tetractys Pythagoras and the Meaning of Number 10

Like The divine number, the holy Tetractys, we find as a symbol expressing god / divine. The number or a symbol: + , 10, used in Ancient Greece, in Ancient China, and within the Kabbalistic Tree of Life, with its ten spheres.

Alchemy Symbols

'Khem is an ancient name for the land of Egypt, and alchemy is one of the two oldest sciences known to the world. The other one is Astrology.'

Manly P. Hall about Alchemy

According to an old Rabbi legend, an angel gave Adam the mysteries and secrets of Kabbalah and of Alchemy, promising that when the human race understand these inspired arts, the curse of the forbidden fruit would be removed and man will again enter into the Garden of Eden.

The earthly body of alchemy symbols is chemistry.

The Phoenicians, and Babylonians were familiar with alchemy. It was the most prized of the secrets of the Atlantean priest-craft, it was practiced in China, Greece and Rome; and it was the master science of the Egypt. The most powerful of the alchemical organizations were the Rosicrucian, the Illuminati, and certain Arabian and Syrian sects.

We will not research the alchemy symbols in depth but attempt to understand its main messages across the cultures, the goals of this sacred science, its practices within the daily life.

What is Alchemy and Nature

Alchemy is based upon the natural phenomenon of growth. According to Alchemists through the self-development the consciousness of man can be transformed from base animal desires (represented by the metals) into a pure, golden, and enlightened consciousness; ignorance can, through proper endeavour and training, be transmuted into wisdom; metals can be transformed into gold.

What is Alchemy?

What is Life according to Alchemy?

What is intelligence? What is the essence? What is Nature of elements?

Nature manifests through growth, it is an urge from within outward, a force that drives expression and manifestation.

It is invisible, it is life found in bodies, animated by the divine breath.

How does the Nature manifest?

Nature manifests as male and female, as Yin and Yang, as Left and Right Sephirot within the Kabbalah's Tree of Life.

Yin Yang Manifestation of Consciousness within Indian Traditional Art

Alchemist must first know the Nature

An alchemist knows that all substances grow from seeds, and that these seeds are already in the body of the substance. Nature transforms the black carbon into diamonds, through millions of years of natural hardening. Alchemy is the Art of increasing and bringing an element into perfection with the greatest possible speed.

The Alchemist must be able to discriminate between the male and female qualities and manifestations. The matter must be separated from its impurities.

Alchemy Symbol, can we give Nature a chemical symbol, a sign, an element?

Nature can be compared to Mercury. Mercury is a chemical element with the symbol Hg and atomic number 80. It is also known as quicksilver. It is highly toxic. Mercury is dual - fixed and volatile, it ascents and descents. Ascending, it seeks to purify.

Alchemy Symbols and Kabbalistic Tarot

Kabbalistic Tarot painted by Oswald Wirth

The stages through which matter passes in its journey towards perfection can be divided into twenty-two parts, the twenty-two major cards of Tarot, twenty-two paths of Kabbalah, and the Twenty-two letters of the Hebrew alphabet.

The Tarot cards are an Alchemical Formula of manifestation.

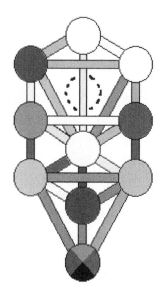

Kabbalah Image of Triad

Alchemy Symbols manifesting in three Worlds

Alchemy preserves the triple key to the gates of eternal life. It is a mystery of manifestation in three worlds: the divine, the human, and the elemental.

The table showing the analogies of the three principles across different cultures and religions from all around the world.

Three principles across different cultures / religions:

Timeless & Eternal	Dynamic & Expanding	Multiplying & Dying; Contracting
Father	Son	Mother / Holy Ghost
Tao	Yang	Yin
Brahma (Creator)	Vishnu (Preserver)	Siva (Destroyer) / Shakti
Kether	Chokmah (Wisdom)	Binah (Understanding)
Spirit	Soul	Body / Mind
Not an element: Life Force, Kundalini, Tao	Fire and Air / Water and Earth	
Philosopher's Mercury	Sulphur	Mercury or Salt

The Alchemist starts with a good seed, puts it to its proper earth, and when the seed is ready s/he rarefies it so that its virtue is increased and indefinitely multiplied. According to Alchemy the Nature should be assisted, so the Alchemist works according to the laws of Nature, recognizing that the Art is merely a method that copies Nature. Within the process of purification the Nature ends...

Alchemy Symbol of Gold

An Alchemist would tell you that all the beings contain in their inmost centre a precious grain of the elementary gold. The nature of man reflects the entire universe in miniature.

According to Alchemy, One is developed into Two, and the two are merged into one. Elementarily and symbolically Sulphur is the living male, and Mercury is the living female. Female and male must be joined together, so that they form a germ. The Alchemist should separate the light from the darkness. Both must be purified and putrefied and joined a-new together. Their merge results in an Egg (Philosopher's Stone) with the four elements joined together. The shell is Earth, the white is Water, the skin between the shell and the white is Air, and the yolk is Fire. In the middle of the yolk there is the 5th element that is the Life Force.

Four elements Ripley Scroll 16th century Alchemy

After the purification, a perfect equilibrium of the four elements enters into the Lapis creating the Philosopher's Stone, the Mercury of the Philosophers, or the Philosopher's Medicine that gives health and cures diseases, perfects metals changing them into Gold. Long life, health, and happiness are all within the promise of this true AURUM, the most powerful and most precious Gold.

Symbolism of Gold

"The golden rule of true occult science: For every one step that you take in the pursuit of higher knowledge, take three steps in the perfection of your own character."

Rudolf Steiner, Knowledge of the Higher Worlds

We constantly seek to materially, mentally and emotionally 'better' ourselves, our-family dynamics, and our society and within this journey we learn about the interconnections of all things, about short-lived happiness and long-term fulfilment, about the ways to treat our Mother Gaia and all the ones that share our little and wonderful planet with us: animals, plants, stones. We constantly learn how to live in harmony with ourselves and the world around us.

Alchemy and Gold

Gold is formed in the centre of the earth, when passing through warm and pure places.

Gold's atomic number is 79. It is a chemical element with the symbol AU (or perhaps AU(M)?) the Latin 'aurum', meaning 'shining dawn' because of its colour.

Gold does not oxidize in air or water and it is one of the least reactive chemical element. Alchemist would say that it contains no life, that it is dead. Gold is entirely free from imperfections. Gold is highly conductive to electricity.

It is believed that most of the Earth's gold lies at its core, the metal's high density made it sink into the Earth's centre. All of the gold found on Earth was deposited later by meteorites that contained Gold.

Spiritual Meaning of Gold

Perfection of own character, whether towards more kindness, more truthfulness, more knowledge and wisdom has been with us humans as our noble goal for 1,000s of years. Excellence is our Inner Gold.

Jung on Alchemy and Gold

"My studies of alchemy may seem obscure and baffle many people, but taken symbolically - the symbolic gold of great worth, or the transforming philosopher's stone 'lapis philosophorum' hunted for centuries by the alchemists - is to be found in man." **C.G. Jung**

"Alchemy represents the projection of a drama both in cosmic and spiritual terms. The opus magnum had two aims: the rescue of the human soul and the salvation of the world..." **Interview of C. G. Jung by Mircea Eliade**

The unique prima materia, the chaos, or the life force from which the "gold" is produced Jung equate to an unconscious content

"The psychological equivalent of this theme is the projection of a highly fascinating unconscious content which, like all such contents, exhibits a numinous – 'divine,' or 'sacred' – quality." **C.G. Jung**

"Practical experience shows us again and again that any prolonged preoccupation with an unknown object acts as an almost irresistible bait for the unconscious to project itself into the unknown nature of the object and to accept the resultant perception, and the interpretation deduced from it, as objective." **C.G. Jung**

The Ancient Egyptians also had a deep connection to Gold. They referred to Ra as a mountain of gold. The Royal Tombs were known as the "Houses of Gold" and the Pharaohs were called the "Golden Horus".

Chinese Alchemy

The ancient science of alchemy still influences the contemporary spiritual theories, and stays shaping the spiritual philosophies of our time.

The whirlpool of its magic at one point became madness for the alchemists who tried to decipher its secret language of symbols and signs, and for the ones who managed to just bath in the beauty of its images, it stayed full of blessings. The desire to knock on the door that promises eternal life and eternal youth returns through centuries to haunt the alchemists with their quest to know the lapis philosophorum, the philosopher's stone - the legendary alchemical substance capable of turning base metals into gold.

Secret of Golden Flower - Merge of Male and Female Energy

It is the merge of male and female that fascinates us so much, it is the White Queen and the Black King that unite to give a birth to a child that is perfect and immortal. It is Taoist Yin and Yang that when circling in perfect harmony create balance and harmony within a Human Being, on Earth and in Universe.

It is Male that is our Collective Consciousness, that is Sun, Reason, Science, Law & Order.

It is Feminine that is symbolised by Moon, or Earth, that is the Ocean of our Collective Sub-Conscious, it is our Dream Consciousness, our shadow existence, trance, dragon and the snake, siren and medusa, that is Life that creates and destroys itself.

The Mind as an unusual Son of Chaos

Mind is symbolised by Mercury, and when Master of its Destiny, his spirit is a hermaphrodite that stands on both: the Sun and the Moon.

Extracts from the Secret of The Golden Flower

In an attempt to further understand this symbolism within our lives we came across an ancient Chinese Alchemy text: The Secret of The Golden Flower, Tai Yi Jin Hua Zong Zhi 太乙金華宗旨, a Chinese Taoist text about meditation, translated by Walter Picca in 1964. The following are some extracts from this Holy Scripture.

It is said that Lao Tzu became one of the Eight Immortals using the methods within this book. The ideas have been traced back to Persia and Zarathustra and the Egyptian Hermetic tradition.

'Master Lao-Tsu said: That which exists through itself is called the Way (Tao). Tao has neither name nor shape. It is the one essence [Hsing], the one primal spirit. Essence and life cannot be seen...

Lao-Tsu

The Golden Flower is the Light. What colour has the light? One uses the Golden Flower as an image. It is the true power of the transcendent Great One...'

About Gold

'The power of the seed, like Heaven and Earth, is subject to mortality, but the primordial spirit is beyond the polar differences. Here is the place whence Heaven and Earth derive their being. When students understand how to grasp the primordial spirit, they overcome the polar opposites of Light and Darkness and tarry no longer in the three worlds.'

About Duality

'In the body is the anima. The anima, having produced consciousness, adheres to it. Consciousness depends for its origin on the anima. The anima is feminine, the substance of consciousness. As long as this consciousness is not interrupted, it continues to beget from generation to generation, and the changes of form of the anima and the transformations of substance are unceasing. But, besides this, there is the animus in which the spirit shelters. The animus lives in the daytime in the eyes; at night it houses in the liver. When living in the eyes, it sees; when housing itself in the liver, it dreams.'

About Consciousness from the Secret Of The Golden Flower

'The one effective, true essence (logos united with life), when it descends into the house of the creative, divides into animus and anima. The animus is in the Heavenly Heart (Mind*). It is of the nature of light; it is the power of lightness and purity. It is that which we have received from the great emptiness, that which has form from the very beginning. The anima partakes of the nature of darkness. It is the power of the heavy and the turbid; it is bound to the bodily, fleshly heart. The animus loves life. The anima seeks death.'

* Chinese Symbol for Heart and Mind is the same

About Anima and Animus

The core Chinese concept is Xin that means both Heart and Mind. This insightful fact shines a wonderful light on any Chinese ancient text and philosophy. The Mind that represents ideas, cognition, and reason, and Heart that represents desires, and emotions, are coming from the same centre and are directed by the same forces. The Xin guides both beliefs and desires. It is the Heart, rather than the brain that is responsible for the belief systems. The Heart is the centre of emotions and desires, or tranquillity and calmness, but also of intellect and understanding.

'Understanding and clarity, knowing and enlightenment, and all motion (of the spirit), are likewise this Light; therefore it is not just something outside the body. The Light-flower of Heaven and earth fills all thousand spaces.'

About Light

'The heart / mind* cannot be influenced directly. Therefore the breathing power is used as a handle...

While sitting, one must, therefore, always keep the heart (mind) quiet and the power concentrated. How can the heart (mind) be made quiet? By breathing. The heart (mind) alone must be conscious of the flowing in and out of the breath; it must not be heard with the ears. If it is not heard, then the breathing is light; if light, it is pure. If it can be heard, then the breathing power is heavy; if heavy, then it is troubled; if it is troubled, then laziness and absent-mindedness develop and one wants to sleep...'

About Breathing Exercises

'If, when there is quiet, the spirit has continuously and uninterruptedly a sense of great gaiety as if intoxicated or freshly bathed, it is a sign that the Light principle in the whole body is harmonious; then the Golden Flower begins to bud. When, furthermore, all openings are quiet, and the silver moon stands in the middle of Heaven, and one has the feeling that the great earth is a world of light and brilliancy, that is a sign that the body of the heart (mind) opens itself to clarity. It is a sign that the Golden Flower is opening...'

About Meditation

'The most important thing in the Great Meaning is the four words: non-action in action. Non-action prevents a person from becoming entangled in form and image (substantiality). Action in non-action prevents a person from sinking into numbing emptiness and a dead nothingness...'

About non-action in action

'As soon as these two substances meet each other, they unite inseparably, and unceasing life begins; it comes and goes, and rises and falls of itself, in the house of primordial power. One is aware of effulgence and infinity. The whole body feels lighter and would like to fly. This is the state of which it is said: Clouds fill the thousand mountains. Gradually it (life) goes here and there quite quietly; it rises and falls imperceptibly. The pulse stands still and breathing stops. This is the moment of true creative unity, the state of which it is said: The moon gathers up the ten thousand waters. In the midst of this darkness, the Heavenly Heart suddenly begins a movement. This is the return of the one Light, the time when the child comes to life.'

About Merge of Yin and Yang

Dionysus, Christians and Neo-Platonism

Dionysius, a Christian monk who in 500 AC, has devoted his life and research to our Mother Philosophy and her Sister Theosophy, in his noble attempt to unite Neo-Platonic Philosophical thought and Christianity with its mystical experience of god or divine.

Known only by his pseudonym, Dionysius, he wrote a series of Greek philosophical essays and for this work he was loved and respected by many. Not able to prove his true name, many a historian and consciousness researcher have gone back to his writings, and as it usually is some have tried to claim the supremacy of his thought, either by plainly copying his concepts or by calling themselves by his-own name.

A large segment of researchers of medieval Christian spirituality do agree with his research and conclusions. For further info check his book: "On the Divine Names", "On the Celestial Hierarchy", and "On Mystical Theology".

God's transcendence or its divinity is essentially experienced as the pair of opposites: being and non-being, time and eternity.

Christians and Mystical Prayer

The human intellect is able to comprehend, or consciously and subconsciously acknowledge God positive, defined with terms: Good, Unity, Beauty, Logos, Life, Wisdom, or Intelligence.

Dionysus writings reflect, and quote, the doctrines of the Pagan philosopher Proclus, who lectured in Athens in 430 AC. His home is believed to have been Syria. The first mention of "Dionysius" (that is the name he gave himself) is in the year 533 AC, when, at a council held in Constantinople, now the capital of the Byzantine Empire, Severus, Patriarch of Antioch, referred to these writings as part of Christian teachings.

They were widely read in the Eastern Church, included into the Commentary of St. Maximus 700 AC, and re-printed within the work of Greek scholars of the 13th and 14th century.

Dionysus' teachings were often quoted by St. Thomas Aquinas within the Western Church.

Dionysus starts with Godhead ὑπερούσιος θεαρχία "Essence" or

"Being" οὐσία as an existence; the highest type materialized on earth. A Super Personal Divine energy, the only kind of consciousness we may attribute to θ + ρ + χ is Universal Consciousness. It is not in its ultimate Nature conscious, nor alive, it is a Super Unity which is neither One nor Many and it forms as Unity and Plurality as ρ + χ.

Godhead is beyond relationships, but it embraces differentiations and relationships with its 7 eternal created activities or Differentiation.

Revelation ἔκφανσις is φ revealing itself. The Ultimate is

incomprehensible, the various Names of God are inadequate symbols of that which transcends thoughts and existence.

The eternally Manifested θ manifests as the Trinity of forces. St. Augustine sees the Trinity belonging to the realm of eternal. They exist "secundum Relativum and not secundum Substantiam."

Not-Being, or the Non-Existent (τὸ μὴ ὄν), the eternal "Nje" (Not in Slavic) manifests within 2 Super Essence streaming eternally. The two Streams flow timelessly with no beginning and no end, and cross, but not mingle, they are timeless and simultaneous. The Streams are Super Essence in Its creative activity. The outer surface is touched and seen corresponding to the Trinity. We may compare the Super Essence to a magnet & the Trinity to its tangible surface, and the two emanating Streams to the positive and negative magnetism at a distance.

The word "Emanation" πρόοδος (PRoBoC in Slavic means Cut Through) is an act by which the Super-Essence goes forth from Itself. The act of

Creation is an ecstasy of Divine Love. The soul must return to the Super Essence by an answering "ecstasy".

There is in the undifferentiated (ὑπερηνωμένη διακρίνεται) ηνωμένη (Slavs would read as NjNŠMeNNj B) Super-Essence that differenciates into the Three Divine Principles of creative Energy, also differentiated into various colours. We got an Emanating Principle or a Person of the Trinity (God or BoG, Xrist or Jesus, H of GHost), and an Emanating Act. All things have two sides to their manifestation: the existence or the Essence and the personality. The principle of a twofold existence underlies all things. The souls possess their true being in each other; a female in a male, the One and the Many, or the Particulars and the Universal. The self centred „Moi" (in Slavic means My), or Personality, is inherently wrong. After the death, the Moi is merged in the Essence as the perfected spirit embracing the two opposite, with the soul that still remains un-merged.

The individuals according to the various laws (λόγοι) of their space and cercumstences are created in this world of Time. The Essence ascends as: Existence, Life, Sensation, Reason, Spirit.

Dionysius discusses Evil showing that nothing is inherently bad. The Super Essenceis is good so evil is ultimately non-existent, It is the nature of zero in mathematics, it makes no difference and yet has an annihilating force since it reduces to zero all numbers that are multiplied by it. That which we call evil is merely a tendency towards nothingness.

The soul is potentially divine, it follows from the ultimate non-entity of evil that, in so far as it exists, it has to be mingled with good. He is writing with an eye on the dualistic heresy of the Manichees at the time. Instead of dividing existent into good and evil, Dionysius proceeds to divide them into "Existent" and "Non-Existent". The process of Creation advances as Life is added to Being, and Consciousness to Life, and Rationality to Consciousness. Concentrating his spiritual powers, man follows Universal stream of Emanation, aNX, and enters into his spirit, becoming unified with the Angels whose creation Dionysius places at the very beggining of the creation.

The mind demands an Absolute Unity beyond this variety of Attributes. The Light is one thing that the human spirit comprehand. This relationship becomes transcended to ecstasy.

Within the second stage of one's understanding of the God's inner nature, the mystical meditative state, where one needs the metaphor of darkness and the sound of Silence, St John tells us all about the nature of contemplative prayer, "light from the divine darkness" and the ecstatic union with Divine.

Medieval philosophy from the fall of the Roman Empire in the 400 AC to the Age of Enlightenment, was closely connected to the Christian theological thought. Both historians and theologians will today agree that in the history of thought, we do find a period that is today known as: John's Age.

The 16th century was a time of great upheaval. Spain, Holland, Portugal have already enjoyed the economic fruits of the colonization, moving their efforts into Asia, Africa, and the countries of the New World. John himself was posted to go for the missionary work in Mexico in the years just before his death.

The church worried about Jews, Bogumils, Muslims, Pagans, and now, Protestants, making them all, the object of concern for the Inquisition.

In 1567, John has finished his studies at the University of Salamanca, and was ordained as a priest of the Carmelite order. His meeting with Teresa of Avila persuaded him that his mission is to work for the reform of the Carmelite order.

John was also imprisoned for his work, he was a spiritual teacher and confessor for the reformed Carmels established by St. Teresa.

John had no sympathy for excessive visions, stigmatizations and the like.

Alchemy and Philosophers Stone Lapis

In search of perfection Mathematics Pi

According to alchemists, the Philosophers' stone (lapis philosophorum) is a substance capable of turning any metal into gold. Also called, the Elixir of the alchemists, it carries the promise of immortality.

Many have tried to find this sacred substance, searching amongst stones, liquids, air, or deep within their soul. The stone that turns metals into gold, the energy that transforms any fire into 'living fire', any flow into 'Divine flow'.

Lapis and VITRIOL

The alchemical motto is: 'Visit the interior of the earth and rectifying (purifying) you will find the hidden stone.'

They sum their knowledge of the 'Path' and the magic of **VITRIOL** within the sentence: ''Visita Interiora Terra Rectificanto Inveniens Occultum Lapidem'.

L'Azoth des Philosophes, Basil Valentine, Paris, 1659.

Alchemy was given a title of an 'Art' and alchemists were the supreme 'Artists' and many gurus and sages tried to decipher the Sacred Art's higher meaning.

Seeking immortality, seeking perfection, Ancient Greeks, Alchemists, Cabbalists, Taoists, Yogis, Mystics of our past experimented with physical manifestations, with their bodies, emotions, thoughts, offering formulas hidden within a vail of images, symbols, mantras, for mystics of the future to contemplate and discover.

VITRIOL by Nuit, Art of 4 Elements (AoL Mindfulness #2)

How high do we need to climb to reach it?

How deep do we need to dig to find it?

Hidden at the very top of the highest Cathedral
Buried at the very bottom of the deepest cave

Concealed at the very top of the Sacred Mountain
Veiled at the very bottom of the Temple's path

Waiting at the very top of the largest pyramid
Rooted at the very bottom of the sacred search

Within the Holy of Holies Sleeps untouched a sparkling pearl
Find it, swallow it & become it and each drop of your blood
Will become a star

Jung, Introduction to the Secret of the Golden Flower

'I know a series of European mandala drawings in which something like a plant seed surrounded by its coverings is shown floating in water, and from the depths below, fire penetrating the seed makes it grow and causes the formation of a large golden flower from within the germinal vesicle. This symbolism refers to a sort of alchemical, process of refuting and ennobling; darkness gives birth to light; out of the 'lead of the water-region' grows the noble gold; what is unconscious becomes conscious in the form of a process of life and growth. (Hindu Kundalini yoga affords a complete analogy.) In this way the union of consciousness and life takes place.'

Tibetan Sand Mandala

Ancient Rome, Wisdom as Lapis

Within this beautiful Latin poem 'Verba Aristei Patris ad filium'

a Roman nobleman Aristei talks to his son about the Art and its Magic Promise:

'What is the use of wealth, when one is liable to be afflicted with human infirmities? Where is the advantage of treasures, when death is about to destroy us? There is no earthly abundance which we are not bound to abandon upon the threshold of the tomb. But it is no longer thus when I am possessed of this Key. Wealth is ever at my command, and I no longer want for treasures; weakness flees away from me; and I can ward off the approach of the destroyer while I own this Golden Key of the Grand Work.

It is by the life that we discern the principle of things; the life of things is the Air, and by consequence Air is their principle. It is for this reason that Air corrupts all things, and even as it gives life, so also it takes it away. Wood, iron, stones, are consumed by fire, and fire cannot subsist but by Air. Now, that which is the cause of corruption is also the cause of generation. There has Nature stored up all her treasures, establishing therein the principles of the generation and corruption of all things, and concealing them as behind special and secret doors. To know how to open these doors with sufficient facility so as to draw upon the radical Air of the Air, is to possess in truth the golden Keys.'

The Secret of Lapis

BY THEOPHRASTUS PARACELSUS: The Aurora of the Philosophers, 1659

'ADAM was the first inventor of arts, because he had knowledge of all things as well after the Fall as before

...they held these arts to be the highest philosophy, to be learnt by their chief nobles and priests. So it was in the time of Moses, when both priests and also physicians were chosen from among the Magi

37

... Magic, indeed, is an art and faculty whereby the elementary bodies, their fruits, properties, virtues, and hidden operations are comprehended. But the cabala, by a subtle understanding of the Scriptures, seems to trace out the way to God for men, to shew them how they may act with Him, and prophesy from Him; for the cabala is full of divine mysteries, even as Magic is full of natural secrets. It teaches of and foretells from the nature of things to come as well as of things present, since its operation consists in knowing the inner constitution of all creatures, of celestial as well as terrestrial bodies: what is latent within them; what are their occult virtues; for what they were originally designed, and with what properties they are endowed.'

Lapis in Kabbalah, Taoism and Yoga

The Esoteric practices of the West mapped within the Kabbalah's Tree of Life were given to posterity in the form of Astrology and Tarot.

Cabbalist Middle Pillar offers the direct path to Divine. The mystics practice various exercises that involve imagination, breath, and concentration, to purify and circulate the life force to be able to better reflect the cosmic energy forces.

In the East, yoga practices were designed to awaken 'Kundalini', the 'Serpent Fire' that sleeps within the bottom of the spine and in China, Taoist experimented with Tao, the Vital Energy, in an attempt to balance Yin and Yang energy manifestation within all the aspects of creation. Taoists Qigong practices work with the human bodies to purify, and circulate the life force.

圖 胎 道

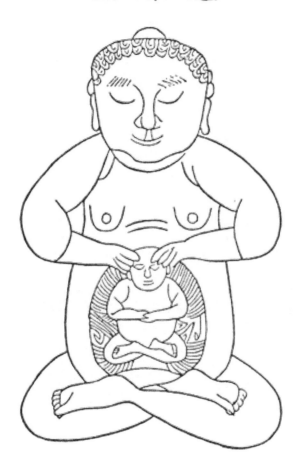

Ancient Chinese Drawing of Chi Gong Practices

Whether Yogis, Pythagoreans, Cabbalists or Taoists, mystics of our past tried to manipulate the chemistry of a human body and create reactions within the mind, offering variety of breathing exercises, yoga exercises, qigong exercises, using sound, symbols and signs, to reach Higher States of Consciousness.

Emerald Tablet of Hermes or Tabula Smaragdina Hermetis

Lapis and The Emerald Tablet of Hermes

The Emerald Tablet of Hermes 'Kitab Balabiyus' is the earliest of all the alchemy works that survives. Hermes, by the Greeks called Trismegistus, an Egypt's King, most probably lived around 400 years before Moses, or around 1900BC.

'This prince, like Solomon, is highly celebrated by antiquity for his wisdom and skill in the secret operations of nature... he is called the Thrice Great Hermes, having the spiritual intelligence of all things in their universal law.'

Mary A. ATWOOD, Introduction to 'Hermetic Philosophy & Alchemy'

The wisdom from the Tablet reached the Western Kings within a Syriac 'Book of Treasures' (9th century) and the 12th century Book of Advice to Kings 'Kitab Sirr al-Asar'. This unique and authentic stone engraved with sacred writings, might be all that has remained from Egypt of her Sacred Art.

The Golden Treatise of Hermes Trismegistus, Concerning the Physical Secret of the Philosopher's Stone, (Excerpts) Translated by A.E. Waite, 1894

"True, without error, certain and most true; that which is above is as that which is below, and that which is below is as that which is above, for performing the miracles of the One Thing; and as all things were from one, by the mediation of one, so all things arose from this one thing by adaptation;

the father of it is the Sun, the mother of it is the Moon; the wind carries it in its belly; the nurse thereof is the Earth.

This is the father of all perfection, or consummation of the whole world.

The power of it is Integral, if it be turned into earth.

Thou shalt separate the earth from the fire, the subtle from the gross, gently with much sagacity; it ascends from earth to heaven, and again descends to earth: and receives the strength of the superiors and of the inferiors - so thou hast the glory of the whole world; therefore let all obscurity flee before thee.

This is the strong fortitude of all fortitudes, overcoming every subtle and penetrating every solid thing. So the world was created. Hence were all wonderful adaptations of which this is the manner.

Therefore I am I called Thrice Great Hermes, having the Three Parts of the philosophy of the whole world. That which I have written is consummated concerning the operation of the Sun".

Lapis and Purification

All of the Mystics recommend that practitioners must purify their emotional, mental, and moral forces.

Purifying, strengthening, and increasing Vital Energy brings a promise of health, wealth and lightness of being.

Lapis by Nuit from Art of 4 Elements (AoL #2)

To release the power of Lapis
    Make the fixed one volatile
And the volatile fixed
    Break Ego and its walls
Cleanse it
    Boil it
      Soften it
Disperse it...
And strengthen the Will
      Descending Divine Qualities
        & your Soul will shine Gold

Pythagoras Music and Numbers

Pythagoras of Samosa was an ancient Ionian Greek philosopher. His teachings influenced the philosophies of Plato, Aristotle, and the Western spirituality.

Born around 570 BC, Pythagoras lived at the same time as Buddha and Lao Tzu and he taught his disciples that a soul goes through an endless wheel of reincarnations until we purify and return to the divine.

Pythagoras formed The Pythagorean Brotherhood, one of the first unpriestly scientific societies teaching philosophy and science. Both men and women were allowed to become members of the order.

Pythagoras teaching holds that every soul is immortal and, upon death, enters into a new body, he is credited with the Pythagorean theorem, Pythagorean tuning, the Theory of Proportions, the sphericity of the Earth, and the identification of the planet Venus. Pythagoras influenced Plato, whose dialogues, especially his Timaeus, are our closest records of Pythagorean teachings. Pythagoras philosophy had a major impact on scientists such as Nicolaus Copernicus, Johannes Kepler, and Isaac Newton. Pythagorean symbolism was used throughout early modern European esotericism.

No authentic writings of Pythagoras have survived.

Like many other important Greek thinkers, Pythagoras was said to have studied in Egypt. Apparently, Pythagoras learned to speak Egyptian from the Pharaoh Amasis II himself, and he studied with the Egyptian priests at Diospolis (Thebes), and that he was the only foreigner ever to be granted the privilege of taking part in their worship. Plutarch (46 – 120 AC) writes in his treatise On Isis and Osiris that, during his visit to Egypt, Pythagoras received instruction from the Egyptian priest Oenuphis of Heliopolis.

According to the Christian theologian Clement of Alexandria (150 – 215 AC), "Pythagoras was a disciple of Soches, an Egyptian archprophet, as well as Plato of Sechnuphis of Heliopolis." Diogenes Laërtius asserts that Pythagoras later visited Crete, where he went to the Cave of Ida with Epimenides.

The Phoenicians are reputed to have taught Pythagoras arithmetic and the Chaldeans to have taught him astronomy.

The Neo-Platonists "sacred discourse" claim that Pythagoras had written the sacred text, spoken by the Orphic priest Aglaophamus. Pythagoras's teachings were definitely influenced by Orphism. Pythagoras and Pherecydes also appear to have shared similar views on the soul and the teaching of metempsychosis.

In Croton

Around 530 BC, when Pythagoras was around forty years old, he left Samos. He arrived in the Greek colony of Croton (today's Crotone, in Calabria) in what was then Magna Graecia. Later biographers tell fantastical stories of the effects of his eloquent speeches in leading the people of Croton to abandon their luxurious and corrupt way of life and devote themselves to the purer system which he came to introduce. According to Porphyry, Pythagoras married Theano, a lady of Crete and had a number of kids.

While he was on Samos, Pythagoras founded a school known as the "semicircle". The school became so renowned that the brightest minds in all of Greece came to Samos to hear Pythagoras teach. Pythagoras himself dwelled in a secret cave, where he studied in private and occasionally held discourses with a few of his close friends.

Metempsychosis or Reincarnation

One of Pythagoras's main doctrines was metempsychosis, the belief in reincarnation. According to Porphyry, Pythagoras taught that the seven Muses were actually the seven planets singing together.

When Pythagoras was asked why humans exist, he said, "to observe the heavens". He practiced divination and prophecy. he usually appears either in his religious or priestly guise, or else as a lawgiver.

"The so-called Pythagoreans, who were the first to take up mathematics, not only advanced this subject, but saturated with it, they fancied that the principles of mathematics were the principles of all things." Aristotle, Metaphysics 350 BC

According to Aristotle, the Pythagoreans used mathematics for solely mystical reasons.

They believed that all things were made of numbers. The number one (the monad) represented the origin of all things and the number two (the dyad) represented matter. The number three, a triangle was the symbol of the god Apollo. The number four signified the four seasons and the four elements. They believed that odd numbers were masculine and that even numbers were feminine,

Ten was regarded as the "perfect number"

Pythagoras believed that the Earth was spherical, and he was the first to divide the globe into five climactic zones

Pythagorean communities existed in Magna Graecia, Phlius, and Thebes during the early fourth century BC.

Aristotle tells us that the philosophy of Plato was heavily dependent on the teachings of the Pythagoreans. Plato's Republic is based on the "tightly organised community of like-minded thinkers" established by Pythagoras at Croton.

The earliest Greek natural philosophies believed that nature expressed itself in ideal forms and was represented by a type (εἶδος), which was mathematically calculated.

Porta Maggiore Basilica in Rome 100 AC

The oldest known Pythagorean Temple is the Porta Maggiore Basilica, a subterranean basilica which was built during the reign of the Roman emperor Nero as a secret place of worship for Pythagoreans. The basilica's apse is in the east and its atrium in the west out of respect for the rising sun.

It has a narrow entrance leading to a small pool where the initiates could purify themselves.

The building is also designed according to Pythagorean numerology, with each table in the sanctuary providing seats for seven people. Three aisles lead to a single altar, symbolizing the three parts of the soul merging with One, the unity of Apollo.

The emperor Hadrian's Pantheon in Rome was also built based on Pythagorean numerology.

Johannes Kepler considered himself to be a Pythagorean. Kepler titled his book on the subject Harmonices Mundi (Harmonics of the World), after the Pythagorean teaching that had inspired him.

Isaac Newton firmly believed in the Pythagorean teaching of the mathematical harmony and order of the universe.

The Sentences of SeXtus

The Sentences of Sextus is an ancient Hellenistic Pythagorean text. The earliest mention of the Sentences is in the mid-3rd century. In history, the work had become attributed to Pope Sixtus (a different person). Sextus was a Pythagorean, who lived in the 100 BC.

"The soul is illuminated by the recollection of deity;

A wise intellect is the mirror of God;

Cast away any part of the body that would cause you not to live abstinently. For it is better to live abstinently without this part than ruinously with it..."

In the 1st century BC, Neo-Pythagoreanism was an attempt to re-introduce a mystical religious element into Hellenistic philosophy.

The Porta Maggiore Basilica where Neo-Pythagoreans held their meetings in the 1st century, in Rome, Italy, was discovered recently, in 1915.

Neo-Pythagoreanism held that union with the divine was possible through ascetic living and contemplation of the cosmic order. The movement of souls to and from the underworld (Orpheus, Sappho) and transitions from one state of being to another (Ganymede, the Dioscuro and Leucippid) on the basilica decorations.

Pythagoras taught that numbers had qualities and that geometric figures were powerful magical symbols.

His institute had three circles of initiates:

The outer circle lived in their own houses, had possessions, and studied at the Institute.

The inner order lived within the society, had no possessions, and were required to be vegetarians.

The third level of initiates were the 'electi' who were initiated in all the spiritual disciplines.

Pythagoras believed that:

- the reality is mathematical in nature
- the earth is round
- that the Soul is immortal, changing from one body to another rising to its union with the Divine

Ancient Greek Numbers / Symbols

Hellenistic mathematicians in the 500 BC, preferred using a system of numbers based on the alphabet. To indicate that a letter is a number, they would place a horizontal line above the symbol.

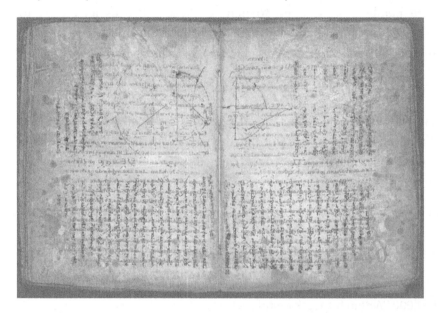

Archimedes Palimpsest 250 BC, an orthodox Christina prayer text 13th century revealed works by Archimedes thought to have been lost

The School of Athens or αθήνα and Numbers with Archimedes of Syracuse

What is now known as "Attic numerals" were in use 700 BC, in the region of Attica, the city of Athens down to the Aegean Sea.

Archimedes of Syracuse or Αρχιμήδης 287 – 212 BC, was an Ancient Greek mathematician, physicist, engineer, inventor, and astronomer, and he is considered one of the greatest mathematician of all time, He was the first to calculate the accurate approximation of pi, defining the spiral bearing his name, he hypotheses that the Earth revolves around the Sun on the circumference of a circle. Archimedes was killed by a Roman soldier, and his original work was "lost" for thousands of years.

The work, also known in Latin as Archimedis Syracusani Arenarius & Dimensio Circuli, is eight pages long in translation, is the Humanity's first mathematical research paper.

Archimedes presents his calculation done for the King, stating that the large numbers were given to him to execute this exciting task, to discover the amount to sand that can fit into the Universe. The Sand Reckoner (Greek: Ψαμμίτης, Psammites) is the name of this work.

Estimating the grains of Sand in Universe Archimade

Can you just imagine the complexity of this task, can you comprehend the advances in science, and the thought form, if the Syracusan king Gelo II, pays the Philosopher Archimedis Syracusani to execute this research and leave it written for the future scientists.

In order to do this, he had to estimate the size of the universe!

Ancient Greek Hellenistic Mathematicians and The Sand Reckoner

Archimedes counts in groups of 10000 (myriad), e.g. 10,0000 instead of 100,000. Within his work he refers to:

1 as "not a number" - for at the time it represented the consciousness going forth to express itself... In the Latin translations it has been translated as "the unit"

The first four numbers symbolized the musica universalis and the Cosmos:

zero dimension

1 = Unity or Monad, a point, supreme God that has not yet materialised

2 = Dyad, one dimension (a line of two points)

3 = Triad, two dimensions, a plane defined by a triangle

4 = Kosmos (Tetrad), a tetrahedron defined by four points

The four rows add up to ten, which was unity of a higher order or the Dekad.

The Tetractys symbolizes the four elements: fire, air, water, and earth

1 unit not a number one of something

8 eight of units that are not a number grouped together

10 Decad ten units grouped together

100 He katontad one hundred somethings

1000 CHiliad one thousand units grouped together

1,0000 Myriad 10,000 units grouped together

Since the Ancient Greek number system is based on the alphabet, symbolically, each Letter has a precise "meaning", "numeral frequency", or "philosophical concept". Archimede for example, speaks of 'one', 'two', 'three', but also of 'first', 'second', third,. for 20 he would use: 2 tens or 2 deka, etc.

His numbers indicate nouns like: monad, dyad, ennead, octad, decad (or decade). These are all philosophical concepts

So, for example, it is wrong to think of an octad as a set of eight units. It is eight units grouped together as a single unit.

This system became the preferred system for Hellenistic mathematicians. This is where all the schools were, in Athens and its Mediterranean surrounding.

There are three sets of 9 numerals from the Ionian alphabet, 24 letters + Supreme Omnipresent God sounds represented as numbers: 6 or Vau, 90 Koppa, 900 Sanpi, the symbols whose sounds today we do not know, for they were hidden by the Priests as sacred.

1,0000 Myriad is 10,000 units grouped together. Knowing that M was later translated into the Latin as 1,000.

In the following list, for their resemblance to the Serbian cyrilic letters symbols, I substituted them with Dj, Dž, Sh. The Cyrillic letters that are unique to Serbian are Ђ (Dj) Ч (CH), Љ (LJ). Њ (NJ) Џ (Dž)

1 A 2 B 3 G 4 D 5 E 6 Ϛ Vau 7 Z 8 H 9 Theta theta

10 I 20 K 30 L 40 M 50 N 60 xi 70 O 80 pi 90 Ϟ *Koppa

100 R 200 S 300 T 400 U 500 phi 600 chi 700 psi 800 omega 900 *Sanpi

Archimedes, The Sand Reckoner Quotes

Archimedes presents us with an answer.

"And so I suppose these concerning the magnitudes and distances, while concerning the sand these. If there is a magnitude composed from the sand not larger than a poppy-seed, the number of it is not larger than ten-thousand, while the diameter of the poppy-seed is not larger than a fortieth-part of an inch..." from Archimedes, The Sand Reckoner

Summary

10000 grains of sand = 1 poppyseed

40 poppy-seeds = 1 inch in length

Hence, 1 inch x 1 inch = 10000 x 40 x 40 = 1600,0000 grains of sand

Can you check is it correct? I can't!

Tetractys Pythagoras and the Meaning of the number 10

Ancient Greek Numbers & Corresponding Letters

Have you ever wonder how the Ancient Greek Numerical system looked like? Knowing the Roman numbers (I II III IV V VI VII VIII IX X MCC) give us an important clue, that the Ancient Greek Numerology must have had alphabetic letters assigned to a number. Manipulating numbers, for our wise ancestors, and ancient philosophers, have also meant, the metaphysics of sounds.

When Ancient Greek Philosophers, and Pythagoras spoke of one (1), two (2), three (3), and four (4) they also spoke of the SOUNDS.

YaHoWa and trinity of hidden sounds.

The number 1 or Alpha narrates a story of "F" not "A". This is a Sacred Symbol "PH" or "F" (Φ in Cyrillic) of both Ancient Egyptians Kings and Priests. The Priests carried Female Sounds (Ha), Kings associated with Male (Ra). The Ancient Greek HeRoDotus writes Data for both Priests and Kings.

The omega tells us of "G" of George. It is interesting that "F" was hidden within the Slavic Languages. Φ gives us a notion of the number 1 that is substance, 2 that is magnitude, motion, line, 3 that defines a surface of the triangle, and 4 that is a 3-dimentional triangle that forms a solid. 1 is more than a "0" that is omnipresent and omnipotent God.

The sacred, hidden, not to be mentioned in vain, name of God "YaHoWa" as a trinity of sounds carries within its 3-ple manifestation into female and male Gods.
Y = manifesting as a trinity of sounds represented within a triangle with Đ + DŽ (J). The 4th that forms a 3-dimentional triangle is Ž. All sounds are Feminine.
H = manifesting as a trinity of sounds represented by a triangle of forces

with X + Č. The 4th Symbol / Sound forming a 3-dimentional triangle is "C"

W = manifesting as a trinity of sounds represented by a triangle of forces with F, M, N, Nj

Ancient Greek numbers and their Symbols

1	α	alpha	10	ι	iota	100	ρ	rho
2	β	beta	20	κ	kappa	200	σ	sigma
3	γ	gamma	30	λ	lambda	300	τ	tau
4	δ	delta	40	μ	mu	400	υ	upsilon
5	ε	epsilon	50	ν	nu	500	φ	phi
6	ς	vau*	60	ξ	xi	600	χ	chi
7	ζ	zeta	70	o	omicron	700	ψ	psi
8	η	eta	80	π	pi	800	ω	omega
9	θ	theta	90	ϙ	koppa*	900	ϡ	sampi

* Vau, koppa, and sampi are obsolete characters

In the ancient and medieval manuscripts, the numerals had a letter + overbars: α, β, γ

In Ancient Greek for example, 241 as 200 + 40 + 1 would have been ΣΜΑ or 666 is written as χξ⬚ (600 + 60 + 6)

Ž Č Š Đ DŽ are inserted by myself, for the comparison of the Ancient Greek Symbols and the Cyrillic letters. The Ancient Greek does not have the hard sounds of Ch, Dž, Zh.

The Tetractys symbolizes the four elements: fire, air, water, and earth
Tetractys κτισις = creation = sounding as ThISiS

The first four numbers for Pythagoras symbolize the musica universalis and the Cosmos:

1 = Unity or Monad, zero dimension (a point)
2 = Dyad, one dimension (a line of two points)
3 = Triad, two dimensions, a plane defined by a triangle
4 = Kosmos (Tetrad), a tetrahedron defined by four points

The four rows add up to ten, which was unity of a higher order or the Dekad.

"Bless us, divine number, thou who generated gods and men! O holy, holy Tetractys, thou that containest the root and source of the eternally flowing creation! For the divine number begins with the profound, pure unity until it comes to the holy four; then it begets the mother of all, the all-comprising, all-bounding, the first-born, the never-swerving, the never-tiring holy ten, the keyholder of all."

The Pythagorean Oath also mentioned the Tetractys:

"By that pure, holy, four lettered name on high, nature's eternal fountain and supply, the parent of all souls that living be, by him, with faith find oath, I swear to thee."

The Tetractys is both a mathematical idea and a metaphysical concept of consciousness.

In ancient Greek religion and mythology, the Muses (Ancient Greek: Μοῦσαι, Moῦsai) are the inspirational goddesses of literature, science, and the arts. They are considered the source of the knowledge embodied in the poetry, lyric songs, and myths that were related orally for centuries in these ancient cultures.

In current English usage, "muse" can refer in general to a person who inspires an artist, musician, or writer. Perhaps the Muses were our first guardians of writing, back in 2,500 BC?

Ancient Egyptian Numbers

You have all heard of the conquest of Alexander the Great in 332 BC, when Ionic Greek (Homer-ian) was the language of the governing classes in Egypt. The Greek ruler, Ptolemy V in 200 BC has commissioned the Rosetta stone, to state publicly that he is the rightful pharaoh of Egypt.

Excavated during the Napoleon conquest of Egypt by French archaeologists, the scholars who had accompanied the French army to Egypt in 1799 AC. It found its way to England, in an exchange of Governments from French to British after the French surrender of Egypt in 1801, and is now in the British Museum... The Rosetta stone is written in three writing scripts: hieroglyphic, demotic, and Greek and it is a block of black granite 115 cm high and 70 cm wide.

Without the Rosetta stone, we would not have been able to decipher the huge amount of writings, scripts, drawings, temples' texts left behind by. The Rosetta stone is in two languages: Egyptian and early Ancient Greek. The writing on the Stone is an official message, a decree, about the king Ptolemy V (204 – 181 BC). The decree was copied on to large stone slabs called stelae, which were put in every temple in Egypt. It says that the priests of a temple in Memphis (in Egypt) supports the king.

This ingénues art-work was carved in three writing systems, hieroglyphic, demotic, and the Greek alphabet and this makes the Rosetta stone one of the most important archaeological discoveries in human history.

The last sentence of the Greek text says, "Written in sacred and native and Greek characters." Scholars identified the "sacred" to the hieroglyphic system, while the "native" referred to the demotic script of the Egyptians.

This is secret and sacred text that has fascinated even Napoleon at the time of his conquest.

When understanding the secret of the language and translations, as a researcher, we got to have in mind that the original deciphering the stone was the work of Thomas Young of England and Jean-François Champollion of France. Thomas Young was very talented and educated men who had Egyptology as hobby in 1814 AC. He correctly identified the name of King Ptolemy, by finding the corresponding name written in Greek.

With our knowledge of Ancient Greek we now know that 3 characters were lost during the transcript to Latin languages, so Ptolemy is the best we could sound we gave to the name of this King. From this he determined which hieroglyphs spelled the name of Ptolemy. This, in turn, gave him the key to the hieroglyphs for p, t, m, y, so P and T within the translations stayed P and T, but could have carried a stronger more defined sounds, more in use in Sacred Rituals of the time.

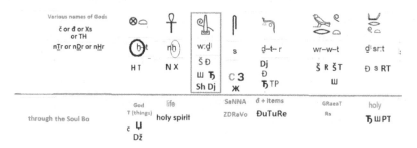

Ancient Egyptian Hieroglyphics for Victory Life Gods Prosperity

Jean-François Champollion, is the founder of scientific Egyptology. An historian and linguist, with the knowledge of French, Latin and Greek and Coptic, the late form of ancient Egyptian that was written phonetically in Greek. Because he understood Coptic he was able to translate the meaning of the ancient Egyptian words.

In 1821 AC, Champollion has brilliantly established an entire list of Egyptian symbols with their Greek equivalents. He tells us, future researchers, that the sacred symbols are both alphabetic and syllabic, and that they also depicted the meaning of the word itself. When studying Chinese, I found the early Chinese characters to have the similar "mission" within their sacred work: to be an alphabetical letter, to be a symbol and to carry a meaning. He also tells us that the Rosetta stone is a translation from the Greek into Egyptian.

He has instigated the science of Egyptology who's letters, written on papyrus, have been buried under the sand for thousands of years in Egypt's dry climate. The ancient Egyptians were possibly the first civilisation to practice the scientific arts. Indeed, the word chemistry is derived from the word Alchemy which is the ancient name for Egypt.

The hieroglyph for 'R'

Ancient Egypt Numbers

Ancient Egyptian numbers 1 to 10 100 1000 10 000 millions

Where the Egyptians really excelled was in applied mathematics.

Hieroglyphic Numbers. The Egyptians had a decimal system using seven different symbols.

1 is a single stroke. All the decimal numbers are represented by the strokes.

10 is a standing circle, Nuit bending from 1 side of the sky to the other.

100 is a spiral, later depicted as a swastika.

1,000 a lotus plant, white moon over a growth.

10,000 is a middle finger, often a symbol of male sexuality in all the worlds cultures.

100,000 is a frog often used for its sexual symbolism in European alchemy, for the resemblance to sperm

1,000,000 is a god (visible as a human being, for other Egyptian gods would have been depicted in a form of an animal or as an invisible – crossed entity) with arms raised above his head.

What is most fascinating is that Egyptians knew about "0" drawing it as an empty column and have used fractions 3,000 years ago.

Orphism in Europe and the Golden Book

An ancient book comprising of six pages of 24 karat gold (measuring 5 x 4.5 centimetres) bound together by gold rings was donated to the Museum by an anonymous 87 year old Bulgarian man from Macedonia who had discovered the treasure in a tomb unearthed 60 years in southwestern Bulgaria. According to Elka Penkova, Head of the museum's archaeology department, the golden book is the oldest complete book in the world, dating to 600 BC.

Etruscan Gold book Thracian prayer 600 BC Bulgaria

The Golden Book is dedicated to the Ancient Greek God of Music Orpheus. This is a funeral book made for an aristocrat of the Orpheus cult.

The most popular cults at these days were the Dionysian mysteries, which came to Greece from Thrace, along with the cult of Orpheus and the Orphic mysteries.

Perperikon in southern Bulgaria is a real city-temple, with the stone altars, dedicated to the God of wine and sexual ecstasy known by the Greeks as Dionysus, or Bacchus by the Romans. Orpheus, the Thracian's musician god, according to legend was a disciple of Dionysus, but had argued against practices of orgies in the name of Apollo, the god of reason. He was murder by the maenads, the female followers of Dionysus. Orpheus death was considered a sacrifice to redeem mankind for its sins.

Some archaeologists believe that Orpheus could have been a real person who resided in the Rhodope Mountains, a Dionysian priest, an initiate of Egyptian mysteries. His cult proclaimed asceticism, was against sacrifice, and taught the transmigration of souls. His followers, including Pythagoras, Plato, Aristotle and Alexander speak of the soul's capacity to experience the divine. The initiated students had learned to break free, resurrect and experience happiness in the afterlife.

According to mythology, Orpheus descended into the underworld to retrieve his dead wife, Eurydice, and did so through the Devil's Throat, a cave in the Rhodope Mountains, of south-eastern Bulgaria. The Greek philosopher Pythagoras is associated with Orphism that has originated in Thracia, in southern Italy and among the neighbouring tribes in Serbia, Bulgaria, Macedonia, Greece.

The golden book full of mystical words and images including a horse, a horseman, a Siren, a lyre, and soldiers has been authenticated by experts in Sofia and London as a genuine 600 BC artefact

Golden Orphism Book is a Thracian golden artefact with total weight of 100 grams. Its contents are related to the Orphism, which existed in the Thracian and Hellenistic world. Illustrations of priests, horse-rider, a mermaid, a harp and soldiers within the golden book is now in the National Historical Museum in Sofia.

Before his trip to the under-world, visit to the dead, Orpheus had been a good musician, but he returned as a prophet and brought the knowledge to the Thracians, centuries before Christ.

Orpheus had to "die" to come back to life transformed. His rituals mention turning water into wine.

The Thracian burial rite images speak of the afterlife and immortality of the soul. The Valley of the Thracian Kings, with over 500 burial hills are in the realm of the Odrisios (500 - 400 BC), ruled by the King III Seuthes. The Thracian funeral rites had many rituals in common with the Egyptian one, especially the idea of resurrection and an afterlife.

The Greek poet Hesiod narrates: "When a husband dies, his wives, which are many for each one, argue in competition... The wife who comes out victorious... will be beheaded by a kin hand over the grave of her husband and is buried beside him, while the ones who lost the case, that is for them the greatest infamy, remain mourning they misfortune".

Ancient Greek Herodotus tell us of the burial practice of breaking favourite items, whatever was destroyed during funeral rites would become useful for the afterlife. Death was considered the beginning of a new life. On this trip, they needed to carry everything they would need. On this trip, they also carried books with the magic inscription to communicate with Gods and spirits.

The Etruscans, one of Europe's most mysterious ancient peoples, have migrated from Lydia, in modern western Turkey, settling in northern Italy nearly 3,000 years ago. They were wiped out by the conquering Romans in the fourth century BC. Yet in the Classical and Hellenistic periods of ancient Greek history, they inhabited the parts of Romania, Bulgaria, Greek Thrace, Turkey, Serbia, the Republic of Macedonia. There were Thracian populations on a number of Aegean islands and in the core territory of Hellas. During the Roman Imperial period, they were in the city of Rome itself and Italy, some were living in Egypt. By the mid 400 BC, Philip II, the king of Macedonia, imposed Macedonian domination over Thrace. The long Roman conquest started by the end of the 200 BC. The ancient Thracian language is almost completely unknown.

We are still waiting for the translation of the Book.

Perhaps it will resemble the Lord's Prayer -

Πάτερ=Father;ἁγιασθήτω τὸ ὄνομά σου=Hallowed be thy Name;

ἐλθέτω ἡ βασιλεία σου=Thy kingdom come;

τὸν ἄρτον ἡμῶν τὸν ἐπιούσιον δίδου ἡμῖν τὸ καθ᾽ ἡμέραν=Give us this day our daily bread;

καὶ ἄφες ἡμῖν τὰς ἁμαρτίας ἡμῶν=And forgive us our trespasses,

καὶ γὰρ αὐτοὶ ἀφίομεν παντὶ ὀφείλοντι ἡμῖν=as we forgive them that trespass against us;

καὶ μὴ εἰσενέγκῃς ἡμᾶς εἰς πειρασμόν=And lead us not into temptation.

Relation to Egyptian Prayer from the Coming Into Day Book of the Dead

There are similarities between the Lord's Prayer and The Judgement of the Dead (Ch.125) in the Egyptian Book of the Dead.

Janzen, W. "Old Testament Ethics" 1994 Westminster/John Knox Press

Address to the gods of the underworld

Hail, gods, who dwell in the house of the Two Truths.

I know you and I know your names.

Let me not fall under your slaughter-knives,

And do not bring my wickedness to Osiris, the god you serve.

Let no evil come to me from you.

Declare me right and true in the presence of Osiris,

Because I have done what is right and true in Egypt.

Or a Greek version -

The Ancient Greek Numerical System Pythagoras and The divine number, the holy holy Tetractys, we find as a symbol express

ὦ Ζεῦ, πάτερ Ζεῦ

 O Zeus, father Zeus,

σὸν μὲν οὐρανοῦ κράτος,

 Yours is the Kingdom of Heaven,

σὺ δ᾽ ἔργ᾽ ἐπ᾽ ἀνθρώπων ὁρᾶις

 and you watch over men's deeds,

λεωργὰ καὶ θεμιστά

 both the crafty and the just,

σοὶ δὲ θηρίων ὕβρις τε καὶ δίκη μέλει.

The Maltese collection of antiques, has an interesting book called Theology, from Albertus, Magnus, Saint, 1193 - 1280, a Dominican from Venice (Italy), reprinted by Ripelin, Hugh, 1270, and Landino, Cristoforo, 1424-1504.

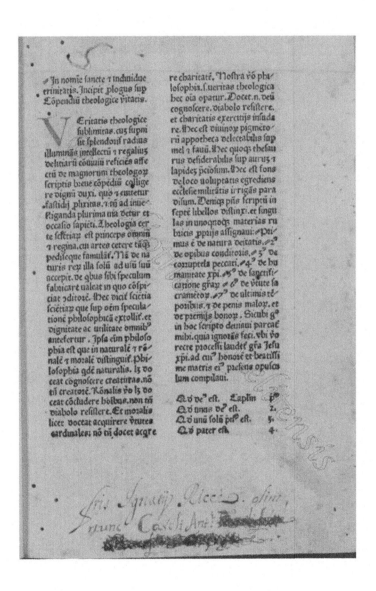

Compendium Theologicae Veritatis Manuscript 1 Malta Public Library Albertus Magnus Saint

In the Middle Ages, this book was considered to be the most widespread manual of Christian theology.

It was distributed, studied, researched, passed from a convent to the other as a Christian thought. Let me tell you why! The work is divided into seven parts treating different theological aspects of the Catholic faith from the Aristotle perspective! I am not joking! It was the famous Aristotle 380 BC that Saint Albert paraphrased. So it was a real treat to see how deep Aristotle philosophy is engraved in the Christian thought!

Within the scientific observations of different types of atoms at similar energy levels, the states with the similar behaviour patterns are called: solid, liquid, gas, and plasma. The Ancient Greek system of Aristotle, a student of Plato attending the Plato's Academy found in 387 BC in Athens, better known as the teacher, advisor, consultant of Alexander the Great who was the first one to travel to Egypt.

Aristotle was appointed as the head of the royal academy of Macedon Kingdom. During Aristotle's time (384–322 BC) in the Macedonian court, he gave lessons not only to Alexander, but also to two other future kings: Ptolemy and Cassander. During the reign of the Argead king Philip II (359–336 BC), for a moment in history Macedonia subdued mainland Greece and Thrace. His son Alexander the Great travelled to North Africa and far East and has died in Babylon in 323 BC in the city he planned to establish as his capital. Alexander's legacy includes the Greco-Buddhism, and the presence of Greek speakers in Persian lands.

Excellence is never an accident It is always the result of high intention, sincere effort, and intelligent execution; it represents the wise choice Aristotle

Excellence is never an accident It is always the result of high intention, sincere effort, and intelligent execution; it represents the wise choice Aristotle

Plato's own most profound philosophical influences are Socrates and Pythagoras. Plato and Pythagoras shared a mystical approach to the soul probably influenced by Orphism.

Albertus Magnus, Saint Albert the Great

Albertus Magnus, also known as Saint Albert the Great or Albert of Cologne, was a German Catholic Dominican friar that during the 13th Century studied Aristotle and Plato and has written philosophical studies synthesising the work of the philosophers of Ancient Greek into the Christian doctrine.

Albert studded at the Italian University of Padua and was a lector at Cologne. Was sent to the University of Paris to complete his theological education and that was the time when he completed his major work. One of his students was believe it or not, St. Thomas Aquinas.

He died in 1280 and was buried in Cologne. In 1931 Pope Pius XI declared Albert a saint.

He paraphrased most of the works of Aristotle. He adopted the Aristotelian philosophical scientific program to prepare a unified theory of medieval Christian intellectual culture. Albert had a strong bias in favour of what we call today "Neo-Platonism".

Together with his student Thomas Aquinas he supported this "natural philosophy" as a Christian philosophical vision.

He wrote commentaries on the Bible, commentaries on all the known works of Aristotle, Albertus undertook as he states "to make intelligible to the Latins" all the branches of natural science, ethics, metaphysics.

Logic of Aristotle's Organon

Albert carefully prepared a paraphrase of Aristotle's Organon (the logical treatises in the Aristotelian corpus).

I was particularly interested in Albert's three-fold distinction, 1-2-3 that had influenced the development of languages, maths, our view of God, its reflection, Goddess and the human Being. Truth vs, corruption, and change. How does one 1 becomes 2, transforming into 3, 4 and 5 that is beyond the mind, yet existing in things as individuated.

Philosophy and Metaphysics

Albert's metaphysics is an adaptation of Aristotelian metaphysics already expressed as Neo-Platonism and Mystical Christianity. He also used the writings of Pseudo-Dionysius to correct some of the Christine doctrine.

The Number 1, Albert calls God, is an absolutely transcendent reality. At the top of this hierarchy of light are spiritual beings, the angelic orders and the intelligences. He adopts the angelic orders as found in Pseudo-Dionysius' treatise of the celestial hierarchy. The intelligences move the cosmic spheres and illuminate the human soul.

In recent decades, the scientists have debated the huge impact of Dionysian thought in later Christian thought, Dionysius's thought historically represented a Neoplatonic approach to theology, and finally because of my huge interest in drawing parallels between the development of languages and psychology

Andrew Louth tells us -

Dionysius/Denys' vision is remarkable because, on the one hand, his understanding of hierarchy makes possible a rich symbolic system in terms of which we can understand God and the cosmos and our place within it...

Albert the Great Quotes -

"The souls possess intellects and are joined to bodies."

„The human intellect is susceptible to illumination by higher cosmic intellects called the "intelligences"."

"Such illumination brings the soul of man into complete harmony with the entire order of creation and constitutes man's natural happiness."

Albert calls the intellect in its final stage of development the "assimilated intellect" (intellectus assimilativus).

"because the divine truth lies beyond our reason we are not able by ourselves to discover it, unless it condescends to infuse itself; for as Augustine says, it is an inner teacher, without whom an external teacher labours aimlessly."

"Divine light is only a means by which the intellect can attain its object."

"But the inner teacher himself is identified with the divine truth, which is the final object and perfection of the human intellect."

"Natural things, he tells us, are received in a natural light, while the things that the intellect contemplates in the order of belief (ad credenda vero) are received in a light that is gratuitous (gratuitum est), and the beatifying realities are received in the light of glory."

"Some [intelligibles] with their light overpower our intellect which is temporal and has continuity. These are like the things that are most manifest in nature which are related to our intellect as the light of the sun or a strong scintillating colour is to the eyes of the bat or the owl. Other [intelligibles] are manifest only through the light of another. These would be like the things which are received in faith from what is primary and true."

But in both natural and supernatural knowing Albert is careful to stress the final object and perfection of the human intellect. This leads naturally to a consideration of Albert's understanding of ethics.

Albert's influence on the development of scholastic philosophy in the thirteenth century was enormous. The philosophers of the Renaissance were attracted to the Albert's expression of Neo-Platonism and his interest in natural science.

The transcendent intelligence is the Logos of Christians. For Plato, however, the Number 1, the realm of perfect forms is indescribable. Within Christian Neoplatonism, or in Ancient Egypt, the transcendent realm of perfect form is personalized, as the Blessed Trinity, God, Son and the Holy Spirit.

What all Christians believe is that goodness, truth, beauty, are rooted in the being of god. Platonic forms pre-exist in the Divine mind.

The angelic choirs circling the abode of God, from Dante's Paradiso, illustrated by Gustave Doré

Date Lost in Translation

"La guerra del Peloponneso, o seconda guerra del Peloponneso per distinguerla da un conflitto antecedente, fu combattuta nell'antica Grecia tra il 431 e il 404 a.C., fra Sparta e Atene, ... Tucidide, V, 11-14" Il 421 a.C. è un anno del V secolo a.C.

In Italian, 421 a.C. is the English 421 BC!!! Imagine that! No wonder it took us, scientists, such a long time to correct arguments based on pure misunderstanding!

The Caduceus

A wand with two serpents twined around it, surmounted by two small wings. the caduceus or magic wand of the Greek god Hermes, Roman Mercury, messenger of gods, protector of Alchemy. The wand represents power and the two snakes wisdom. The Greek Hermes found his analogue in Egypt as the ancient Wisdom God Thoth, as Taaut of the Phoenicians, all linked with the magic rod with twin snakes.

The Rod of Asclepius and Medical Symbolism

The Rod of Asclepius is a rod with one snake coiled around it and it belongs to the god Asciepius. Asclepius is described in Homer's Iliad, so he was most probably a physician who practised in Greece around 1200BC. Later he became known as the Greek god of Healing. Around 300 BC the cult of Asclepius was very popular and healing temples were many. A particular type of non-poisonous snake was used in healing rituals and the ritual purification.

To heal the sick would spend the night in the holiest part of the temple. Asclepius is traditionally depicted as a bearded man holding a staff with one sacred serpent coiled around it. The worship of Asclepius spread to Rome and continued to the sixth century.

Occult Hermetic Symbolism

Alchemists became known as the sons of Hermes or 'practitioners of the hermetic arts'. By the sixteenth century, the study of alchemy includes medicine, chemistry, and the knowledge of metals.

The caduceus represents the integration of 4 elements: the wand for the earth, the wings for the air, he snakes for the fire and serpents movement for the water.

An occult description refers to Hindu Yogic knowledge of Ida and Pingala, male and female kundalini force as it moves through the chakras and around the spine to the head represented by wings of Mercury. The central rod is Sushumna passing through the spine to the pineal gland into altered states of consciousness. The symmetrical arrangements of two snakes symbolize the moving opposing forces balancing one another creating a higher static form.

Nagakals in India: Healing Snakes

Nagakalas are sacred snakes worshiped as a symbol engraved on stones in India. Intertwining serpents are considered to be a symbol of the god who cures all illnesses. Note the stone on the left and how closely it resembles the Caduceus with 2 snakes rising in between a wand and a bird like wings on the top of the wand.

Symbolism of Caduceus in Bible: Old Testament

"And the Lord said unto him [Moses], what is that in thine hand? And he said, A rod. And he said, Cast it on the ground. And he cast it on the ground, and it became a serpent; and Moses fled from before it. And the Lord said unto Moses, Put forth thine hand, and take it by the tail. And he put forth his hand and caught it and it became a rod in his hand." Exodus 4:2-4

And the Lord said unto Moses, "Make thee a fiery serpent, and set it upon a pole: and it shall come to pass, that every one that is bitten [by a serpent], when he looketh upon it, shall live." Numbers 21:8.

Cadmus fighting the dragon Amphora from Euboea 550 BC Louvre

To the Serpent, by Nuit, from Art of 4 Elements (AoL #2)

So much celebrated, so much cursed
Serpent of Garden of Eden
Life that goes Forth
With the Knowledge of Good and Evil

Life that multiplies and destroys everything It touches
Life that is: Consciousness
That goes forth to-wards Divine
Through the Tree of Life and its SeFirots
Through the Yi Jing transformations
Through Shiva and Shakti's dance on the floor of Maya

To the trinity of Father / Son / Holy Spirit
To Sat / Chit / Ananda
To Kether / Binah / Chokhmah
To the ascent above the Abyss

The Serpent that flows through
Sushuma-to-Sahasrara
Kundalini, Qi, Life Force

I follow Your Wisdom

Mellieha chapel Madonna

Spiral Symbolism

Spiral is mystical, spiral is magical, spiral is an ancient symbol of Divine.

Embedded within the Universal pattern of Galaxies and also engraved within each tiny shell, it fascinated many from the beginning of times.

The spiral is within the strands of our DNA, flower petals, the branching of trees, a spiral shell, and the shape of our galaxy.

Spiral and Golden Ratio

The Golden Ratio, roughly equals to 1.618, was first formally introduced by Pythagoras. Plato (428 B.C. - 347 B.C.) considered the Golden ratio - Fibonacci numbers - to be the most universally binding of all the mathematical relationships.

The Golden ratio, the Fibonacci sequence runs 1, 1, 2, 3, 5, 8, 13... (each subsequent number is the sum of the two preceding ones) is found everywhere in nature and it is related to the Golden spiral, that often shapes our concept of proportion and beauty. The Golden Mean represented by the Greek letter 'phi' is one of those mysterious natural numbers that appears regularly when life grows and unfolds in steps.

The pattern can be found in the placement of the leaves on most plants, in a pine cone, in the shape of our DNA, in distant galaxies reflecting the magic interconnectedness of our micro and macro cosmos.

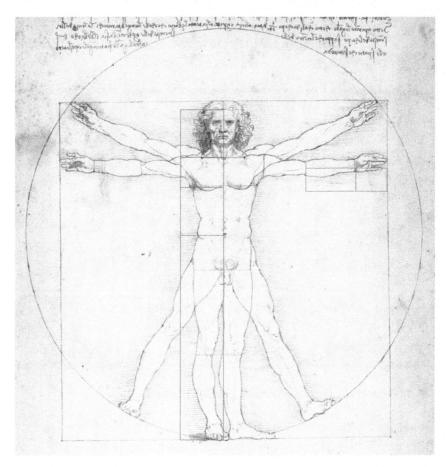

Leonardo da Vinci's 'Vitruvian Man' (1487) illustrates the Golden ratio.

The drawing is based on the correlations of ideal human proportions with geometry. He examined the human body in relation with the square (material existence) and the circle (spiritual existence).

Da Vinci deliberately used the Golden ratio to define all of the proportions in his Last Supper and his Mona Lisa.

Ancient Spiral and its Cosmic Symbolism

Ancient spirals are engraved in Ancient Mayan Temples, in Temples found in Malta that are the oldest free-standing temples on Earth (built around 5,000BC), in Egypt, in India as engravings of Kundalini serpents spiralling up, in China as a symbol for the sun.

Malta Neolithic Temples Tarxien Spirals 2,700 BC

Found within the oldest temples across our little planet it narrates a story of our search towards infinite, our path to consciousness. From the centre to the infinite end, looking at the spiral we see and feel the expansion that spiral carries within its symbolism.

From unit consciousness to divine consciousness, from point to infinity symbolising the journey of our souls. 'The spiral is a spiritualized circle. In the spiral form, the circle, uncoiled, has ceased to be vicious; it has been set free.' **Vladimir Nabukov, About Spiral**

'Progress has not followed a straight ascending line, but a spiral with rhythms of progress and retrogression, of evolution and dissolution.'

Johann Wolfgang von Goethe

'The spiral is an archetypal symbol that represents cosmic force.'

Carl Jung

Seashell Spirit Wish, by Nuit from Art of 4 Elements (AoL Book #2)

And on the 7th day Seashell Spirit made a wish
To be One and All With God
Either as a dot or an infinite end...

And God was so touched
That She said:

Ocean frames your beauty
and sea whispers in your depths
Your spiral will be the code of knowing me

That is why I will:
- Give you birth within a man -
Circling endlessly through life and death
In search of the key to my Heaven's door

And I will:
- Give you birth as Universe-
Spiralling freely through space
Mapping my wisdom through its dance

And I will:
- Give you birth as Self awareness -
Hidden within the DNA of all my Life
And through it you will stay

My secret, my seed, my tetragrammaton

Spiral of Life or Trinity

Trinity Around the World: Symbols for Trinity

The principle of trinity is found in all the world's religions.

Spiral of Life and Trinity Spiral are mystical symbols of trinity

'Spiral of Life' represents:

- Unity of body, mind and spirit.
- Interplay of birth, growth, and death

It is a symbolic representation of primordial forces that materialize in magical, mysterious fashion while obeying precise universal laws.

Ancient Spiral found in Temples

Ancient Tree of Life starts with a Triad

From this primordial triangle proceed all of the other figures, shapes, forms, all other numbers, the magic of manifestation.

Christian Holy Trinity

The Christian Holy Trinity is seen as: God the Father, God the Holy Spirit, God the Son or Christ Consciousness

Symbolism of Trinity in Christianity

Within the Christian teachings Holy Trinity is worshiped through a number of rituals:

Worship and praise are offered 'to God through Jesus Christ in the Holy Spirit'

Blessings and baptisms are given 'In the name of the Father and of the Son and of the Holy Spirit'

Prayers are given to three-in-one. 'Glory be to the Father, and to the Son, and to the Holy Ghost; As it was in the beginning, is now, and ever shall be, World without end. Amen'

The Trinity also expresses the way Christians relate to God:

- worshiping the Father
- following the example given by the Son

- acknowledging the Holy Spirit that lives in each and every of us

The doctrine of Christian Trinity resembles the Hindhu Trimurti where Brahman is also Brahma, Vishnu and Shiva, yet all three are ultimately Brahman.

Hindu Trinity Doctrine: Trimurti

Trimurti Hindu Trinity Traditional Image

The three major Hindu Gods are Brahma, Vishnu and Siva - Creator, Sustenance and Destroyer.

The Hindu Trinity represents the Divine in its threefold nature.

Each part of the Trinity contains and includes the others.

Each God in the trinity: Brahma, Vishnu and Shiva has his Goddess. Brahma's consort is Saraswati, the Goddess of knowledge; Vishnu's is Lakshmi, the Goddess of delight, beauty and love, and Shiva's is Parvati (or Kali or Shakti), the Goddess of transformation, and destruction.

The Hindu trinity's origin can be also found in Babylon, where it might have been incorporated into the Kabbalah, with the Jewish names of the 'sephiroths'.

Supernal Triad within Kabbala

The Supernal Trad within Kabb(h)ala's Tree of Life of Kether (Divine Consciousness), Chokmah (the Son in relation to Kether as its Father, it is the active, male principle of existence) and Binah that embodies the primal female energies. Under this trinity is the Abyss with the rest of the manifestation.

Above the Abyss is the realm of ideas. Kether represents the initial spark, Chokmah is the flame that extends out, and Binah holds the flame. Chokmah and Binah are El and Eloha, the creator God and Goddess of Kabbalah, together in Divine Union they are Elohim. Kether is neither masculine nor feminine, it just is.

Before the beginning of creation there was only En Sof. En Sof was everything, and no-thing. As the energy of En Sof became a concentrated spark of light, it became Kether (the Source). In the same instant, there was energy moving in all directions (the Big Bang). This dynamic expansion is Chokmah (Life Force). The energy is channelled following precise Universal laws towards manifestation. This womb that channels and directs the light is Binah (Primordial Mother).

Other Trinity Dc / Doctrines

We find the concept of trinity in many other beliefs systems:

- the Egyptian Trinity of a transcendental god Amun that also manifests as Ra and Ptah. Of God Ra that has a daughter Maat (Wisdom, Knowledge) that is a consort or sister of God Thoth (Divine Word or Logos of Ra). This was soon replaced with Osiris, Isis and Horus.

- the Greek Trinity consisting of Zeus (the God), Hera (the Goddess) and Hercules (their son) / Athena (their daughter)

- the Babylonian Holy Trinity consisting of Ninki (later became Ishtar) the mother, Enki (later became Namakh) the father, and

Marduk the son. Three animal icons associated with the three Sun 'gods' are: the lion for the goddess, the bull for the father, and dragon for the son.

The three sacred Vedic energy manifestations – Tamas (inertia, darkness, destruction), Rajas (preservation, movement, dynamic), and Satvas (creation, existence, order, purity)

Tao that manifests as Yin and Yang

Spiritual Meaning of Numbers and Ancient Egypt

In search of Perfection Music & Numbers Maxim Vengerov

'Numbers and numerical proportions have a certain meaning for the cosmos and the world. It is in numbers, we might say, that the harmony that dwells through space is expressed'

Rudolf Steiner, Occult Signs and Symbols

Writing was believed to have been given to humanity by the Egyptian god Thoth Thōth (Θώθ). Thoth, lord of ritual and of words, is an Egyptian god who gave us writing. Plato mentions Thoth in his dialogue Phaedrus. He says writing is a wonderful substitute for memory, yet it will cause that the future generations will hear much without being properly taught, and will appear wise but not be so. Thoth gave us the ancient Egyptian symbols wisdom of the frequency of the 22 letters and sounds, possibly through the mystical learnings passed through the centuries through the Tarot cards and Kabbala's Tree of Life.

Another Thoth, the Ancient Egyptian King Tut-ankh-amun and his carved letters, left a deep cultural and scientific impact on the history of European / Arabic writing. His carved letters / books are today known as Amarna Letters and speak of writing as a skill much before 1,400 BC.

In 1887, a local Egyptian woman has uncovered a cache of over 350 stone carved tablets written in cuneiform. From 382 tablets: to be precise, 350 were letters. over 40 of them were discussing legal matters and they speak of the religious reform led by this Egyptian Ruler: to Babylonia, to Assyria, to Mittani, to Arzawa, Alashia and Hatti. Today, these most ancient, carved in stone booklets are scattered in the museums all over the world. Just for the history lovers, the timing does correspond to the timing of Moshes 10 commandments (around 1400 BC). Several letters date back to the rule of Akhenaten's father, Amenhotep III (1390 – 1353 BC), were among those found at Amarna.

1360 BC Akkadian diplomatic letter found in Tell Amarna diplomatic correspondence between the Egyptian administration and its representatives in Canaan and Amurru during the New Kingdom

Tut-ankh-amun's tomb was discovered in the Valley of the Kings, near Luxor, Egypt, in 1922, by the British archaeologists. It is the only tomb dating from the pharaonic New Kingdom (1550 BC – 1069 BC) to be found intact. The Valley of the Kings is a desolate wasteland utterly devoid of vegetation covered by desert.

The tomb of young pharaoh Tut-AnX-Amun was hidden underneath the remains of workmen's huts built during the later Period. Said to "cursed", his tomb "hid" a secret within its walls. For the superstitious many, "Do not enter, or use your mind, for you will be "cursed"".

Writing Amarna Tablets about AΘen from Tut-AXen-aten

Akhenaten (note the possible pronunciation aXeN-aTeN / Nj), 1378 - 1361 BC, was the first Egyptian ruler in history, who has specifically written about Egyptian Gods, a practice usually kept behind the close doors of the temples. The deity called Aten inspired such devotion in Pharaoh Akhanaten that he built a new capital city which he named 'Horizon of the Aten' (modern Amarna), dedicated to the AΘen. He spoke of a deity with no image, an omnipotent God/ goddess that emanates aNX, holy spirits, served by all the other Ancient Egyptian Gods, as the ancient saints or angels, who all had their own role in the kingdom of God.

Amarna Letters paint an interesting picture of Ancient Egyptian Rulership but more specifically speak of writing as a practice that was well established during their time. "To the King, My Sun, My God, the Breath of My Life…" This remarkable collection contains requests for gold, offers of marriage, warning of a traitor, and promises of loyalty to the pharaoh – letters of correspondence, all written in Akkadin. The Amorite tribes from Babylonia, the beginning of the 2,000 BC, used this ancient language structure that had the letters still used in Arabic or with Balkan Slavs – ć, č, š, ž, đ, dž, nj – like in my name Nataša Pantović.

Ancient Egyptians have introduced a belief in resurrection, and life after death was their big story, so "becoming Osiris" or re-incarnating through Holy Spirit or aNX is on many Ancient Egyptian tomb paintings.

LETTER CHART

LATIN	HEBREW	ARAMAIC	GREEK	Cyrilic
B beth	⅁	⊐ beta	B	Б
G gimel	٦	⅂ gamma	Γ	Γ
D daleth	◁	⅂ delta	Δ	Д T/D
(Dj)				(Ђ Ǵ)
S samek	≢	ʊ xei	Ξ	Ж Ž
Z zayin	Σ	Ꭵ zeta	Z	З
(T) teth	⊗	℧ theta	Θ	Ф F PH

Mo-She (Moses)
1050 Icon, Sinai

ARTOF4ELEMENTS.COM

These twenty-four letters are: Α α, B
β, Γ γ, Δ δ, Ε ε, Ζ ζ, Η η, Θ θ, Ι ι, Κ κ, Λ λ,
Μ μ, Ν ν, Ξ ξ, Ο ο, Π π, Ρ ρ, Σ σ/ς, Τ τ, Υ υ,
Φ φ, Χ χ, Ψ ψ, and Ω ω.

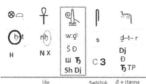

Old Geeze & AmHaric
symbol for Theta ➡ (m)

LATIN	HEBREW	ARAMAIC	GREEK	Cyrilic
E/A ayin	O	У omega	Ω	Ц
SH shin	(W)	ⱳ sigma	Σ	Ш
R resh	◁	⅂ rho	P	P
H (T) tau	X	⊓ tau	Τ	X

ARHaNDjeo GAVRiNa
12th century Hilandar

Various names of Gods
 č or đ or Xs
or TH
nTr or nDr or nHr

Rossetta Stone, Egypt - Symbols from Egypt

⊗	☥	🖉	‖	⌇
(h)t	nb	w:dj	s	d-t-r
H	N X	Š Đ	C З	Dj
		Ш Ђ		Đ
		Sh Dj		Ђ TP
	life	SaNNA	d + items	
	HuMaN	ZDRaVo	ĐuTuRe	
	ČoNo			

SPHING of NeXoS
660BC, Delphi

IW
Ш
Ꭶ

Great SPHiNG of GZiRa, Egypt

St Jovan protector of Sh Christian
Orthodox Icon 12th century, Hilandar

86

The items always found in the tombs are the ancient Egyptian funerary texts. The text incorporates the ancient Egyptian Book of the Dead. As early as 3000 BC, the Royal pyramids contained the Pyramid Texts, carved especially for the pharaoh and as early as 2500 BC the Coffin Texts, developed from the Pyramid Texts were painted on the coffins.

The Ancient Egyptian Negative Confessions

The Ancient Egyptian Negative Confessions written on Temple walls and burial texts were "I have not stolen...", "I have not killed", etc., a letter written to Gods, engraved on Temples walls and prepared as Papyruses 2,000 BC and were equal to "Thou shalt not", the Ten Commandments of Jewish and Christian ethics, later perceived as divine revelation. The Negative Confession was accompanied by a list of protective sounds and symbols that kept souls safe from demons.

Ahmed Osman about Tut-Ankh-Amun Trinity and Jesus

A historian, lecturer, researcher and author, Ahmed Osman is a British Egyptologist born in Cairo who published three books: Stranger in the Valley of the Kings (1987), Moses: Pharaoh of Egypt (1990) and The House of the Messiah (1992) says that Tut-Ankh-Amun had a very similar "story" to Jesus.

"In the tomb of Tut-Ankh-Amun (*note the name TuT aNX aMN) there is a unique scene, not found in any other Egyptian burial, representing the Trinity of Christ. As I stood alone, gazing at the painting of the burial chamber on the north wall, I realized for the first time that I was looking at the strongest pictorial evidence linking Tutankhamun and Christ." He tells us.

"The painting is divided into three separate scenes... It was the ultimate scene on the left of the north wall, however, that aroused my wonder. Here I saw three different representations of Tutankhamun linked as one person. On the left of the scene stood Tutankhamun as the risen Osiris, with a second Tutankhamun facing him as the ruling king, Horus. Behind him is a third Tutankhamun depicted as his Ka." Ka is Soul.

Pharaoh Tutankhamun Tomb, Ancient Egypt 18th dynasty North Wall

"The most remarkable feature of this scene is the fact that the risen Osiris, although shown in the conventional mummified form with his hands folded across his chest, is reaching out to touch Horus, as is his Ka. Thus we have Tutankhamun as father, son and spirit — the same relationship that we find in the Christian Trinity of the three persons in one God — Father, Son and Holy Spirit — finally established as orthodox belief after much acrimonious debate during the first four centuries of the Christian era."

Osman explains "Until the end of the fourth century AC Christian pilgrims came to Egypt and the Christian cross was the Key of Life, the ANX. Christianity was the last phase of the Osirian Cult. Resurrection is originally an Egyptian concept. Indeed, resurrection was the central focus of Egyptian religion."

Tutankhamun NebKheperU-Ra

Winged scarab of Tutankhamun with semi-precious stones. This pectoral is composed of Tut's Prenomen name: "NebKheperU-Ra", the hieroglyphs of: Basket, Scarab-(in Plural-strokes), and Re.

Deus, θεὸς, Gott, or Bog, or NeBo

In Ancient Mediterranean God was called variants of Deus, θεὸς, in others of Gott, or of Bog, or of NeBo thus defining the Romance, Germanic and Slavic language families. As early as the sixteenth century, European priests had noticed similarities between Sanskrit and European languages. But, Sanskrit was knocked from its pedestal as the original mother tongue by the professionals. So this left us with

Gospel of John found in Egypt 200 AC

In the oldest preserved Gospel of John found in Egypt 200 AC we hear the famous:

"In the beginning was the Word, and the Word was with God, and the Word was God…"

Following the Ancient Greek Ionic pronunciation we read:

Ἐν ἀρχῇ ἦν ὁ λόγος καὶ ὁ λόγος ἦν πρὸς τὸν θεόν καὶ θεὸς ἦν ὁ λόγος.

En arkhêi ên ho lógos kaì ho lógos ên pròs tòn theón kaì theòs ên ho lógos.

N aRČe / aRXe + H ἦν (NjM) H LoGoS, kaì ho lógos ἦν pròs tòn θεόn, καὶ θεὸς ἦν ὁ λόγος.

* πρὸς *prosi – in Slavic "say" τὸν *sound (in Slavic "ton", meaning "sound")

θεόν, θεoN, and θεὸς ἦν *god / goddess

oN, thought to be a name of Osiris is also a symbol for Gold

Pythagoras gave the name of Monad (1) to God, and Dyad (2) to matter. The first and highest aspect of God is described by Plato as the One. The Monad (indescribable) emanated the Demiurge (Tao, Consciousness, and Transcendent Source) or the creator. Plotinus who is noted as the founder of Neoplatonism metaphorically identified the Demiurge as the Greek God Zeus θευς.

Ancient Egyptian creation myths appear first in the Pyramid Texts, tomb wall decorations and writings, dating back to the Old Kingdom 2780 BC – 2250 BC.

The world had arisen out of the lifeless waters of chaos, called Nu, NoĆ in Slavic. The god Nu had his female counterpart Nun.et (NuT) represented as the inert primeval water itself; male HuH and his female counterpart Huh.et represented space, H of the AlaH; Kek and Kauk.et disperse the darkness with knowledge; and Amun and Amaun.et represented its hidden nature (Amin, Amen, Amon or perhaps ἦν the Ancient Greek non-existent).

The Tree of Life, Tarot and the Four Elements

When analysing numbers and the mystery of Kabbalah and Tarot we must remember that in Europe in 12th century Tarot was as common as a pack of playing cards.

Among the principle elements of Qabalah, we find:

10 sephiroth, or categories of manifestation, each existing in four Worlds reflected within the Minor Arcana within Tarot: 10 numbered cards each existing in four suits.

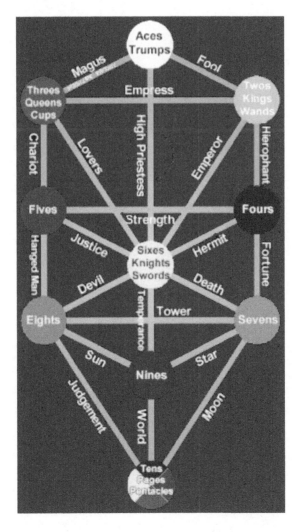

The four suits correspond to the four letters of the Divine Name Hwhy, Yod Heh Vav Heh, to the four elements of the alchemist, and to the four Qabalistic Worlds.

- Disks, Earth, Physical-Material, the World of Action H Heh Daughter

- Wands Fire the Archetypal World (Mental) y Yod Father

- Cups Water the Creative World (Emotional) h Heh Mother

- Swords Air the Formative World (Astral-Psychological) w Vav Son

The Knights represent the power of letter Yod. They are the most sublime, original and active energy of the element: lightening, rain, wind and mountains.

The Queens represent the letter Heh. They receive, ferment and transmit the energy of their Knight.

The Princes represent the forces of letter Vau. A son carrying the combined energies of his parents. He is the intellectual image of their union.

The Princesses represent the forces of He. They represent the energy sent forth in its completion, its crystallization.

Pythagoras Numbers and their Divine Power

Starting with a point that is symbolically the centre, the seed, the source and drawing a circle around it we get the symbol called the Monad. The Monad represents the number one. The Monad is also called Essence, Foundation, and Unity. Pythagoras believed the Monad to be God.

Contemplating itself, the circle becomes two. Creating a line that connects the two centres of the circles is called Dyad. Greek philosophers believed that the Dyad divides and unites.

The equilateral triangle represents the Triad. The triad symbolises wisdom, peace, and harmony because the triangle represents balance, stability and strength.

Tetrad is a shape of a square that exists within the circle. Four symbolises completion.

Pentad is the shape of the star. The pentad was used as a secret sign among the Pythagoreans.

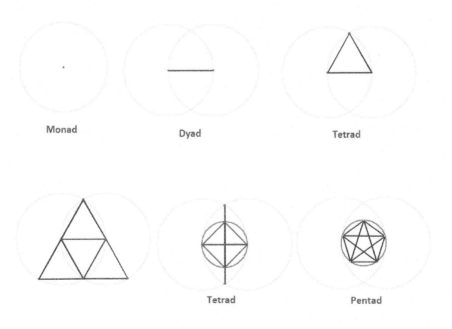

Monad

Dyad

Tetrad

Tetrad

Pentad

The image of the pentad is found in nature in leaves and flowers. The Greeks believed each point of the pentad to represent an element: water, earth, air, fire, and idea.

The Decad represents the number ten. Symbolizing both material world and heaven, the Decad is our formula of the creation of the universe.

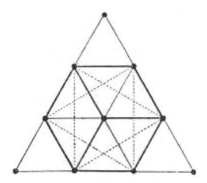

Tetractys Pythagoras the meaning of number 10 ten

The Symbolism of Zero 0

It took Europe relatively long to accept the concept of zero. Accepting zero, enlightened minds of the time finally acknowledged the possibility of an idea that has no form and does not exist. For some Monastic Orders Zero provided a framework for the development of atheism.

Zero is associated with nil, non-being, nothingness, emptiness, and with zero defining non-quantitative as non-existent, everything non-quantifiable could now be defined as non-existent - including God.

Accepting zero led to the invention of relative numbers, negative quantities, infinite decimal points, abstract and irrational, imaginary numbers. It led to the birth of complex mathematics.

0 is symbolised by the Tarot card called: Fool, the Element of Air

It is represented by the HEBREW LETTER: Aleph = Bull or Ox. It is the sound of free breath, unstructured, unconditioned Silence, Tao of Taoists or Kundalini Life Force of Hindus.

Spiritual Meaning of Number One 1

John the Baptist (c. 1513–16), Leonardo's da Vinci's depiction of 1

John the Baptist 1516 Leonardo da Vinci

The number one 1 is represented by the Tarot Card called The Juggler, the Hebrew letter Beth = House represented by Mercury that is action in all forms.

The Aces are the 'root' principles of each element. Mercury represents Spirit ruling the four elements. Within the Tree of life in Kabballah Spirit represents Kether.

'Energy sent forth. This card therefore represents the Wisdom, the Will, the Word, the Logos by whom the worlds were created.' **Crowley**

Egyptian Symbolism of Number 1

1 in Egypt appears as a symbol of individuality. The creator god, oneness that becomes many.

Chinese Spiritual Meaning of Number 1

In China the number 1 yi is an auspicious number. One has the energy of the initiation, new growth and new potential. It is a prime Yang number. The one represents the horizon or heavens.

Spiritual Meaning of Number Two 2

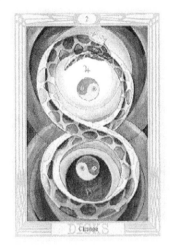

Tree of Life Tarot and Number Two

Kabbalah gimel 2 is represented by the Tarot Card called High Priestess, it is Hebrew letter Gimel = Camel. Ruled by the Moon, the female symbol.

The Crowley Tarot Card Two represents the possibility of form. The elements appear in their original harmonious condition.

Within the Tarot symbolism the energy of fire (wands) is represented in its best and highest form as: Lord of Dominion.

The energy of water (cups) is manifested within all its beauty as: Lord of Love.

The energy of air (swords) is represented as Lord of Peace.

The two of Pentacles represent the energy of Earth, and are called the

Lord of Harmonious Change.

Egypt Symbolism of Number Two

In Egypt: 2 is the number of duality and unity, harmonized opposites, the two eyes of the god of heaven. Heaven is a female and the gods of the earth are male. It is unity rather than diversity that is emphasised in the Egyptian art.

China Symbolic Meaning of Number Two

The number 2 二 èr is the prime Yin or feminine number that represents balance.

Two is one doubled, mirrored, reflected within the state of harmony.

Spiritual Meaning of Number Three 3

A fairly early monotheistic notion, of one and supreme divine, was evident within the development of the languages, and it in its puzzling complexity narrates the mystical story of the Holy Trinity. In Babylonian astrology 2,000 BC, we find the triad of Sun-Moon-Venus. The Star of three Divinities: Ishtar of Akkad, Ishtar of Uruk and Ishhara. Ishtar of Akkad: Morning Venus, Ishtar of Uruk: Evening Venus and Ishhara: Invisible Venus. Elaborate tables were prepared to show her distinction as an evening, morning star or an invisible planet. The moon, as En-Zu, "the lord of wisdom" in astrological texts Sin always takes over Shamash, the sun-god. Jupiter was identified with Bel-Marduk as the chief god of the pantheon.

Often as a metaphysical and mathematical concept used within Ancient Egyptian images, symbolism, writing as far back as 2,500 BC. Preserved in Europe through Ancient Greeks philosophy of numbers and through writings, rituals, prayer. Each Ancient Egyptian book of Dead would start with a sentence exploring the creation of the world, cosmos, universe, sounds, frequencies, numbers, and gods' names.

Pythagoras gave the name of Monad (1) to God, and Dyad (2) to matter. The Monad (indescribable) emanated the Demiurge (Tao, Consciousness, and Transcendent Source) or the creator. Plotinus who is noted as the founder of Neoplatonism metaphorically identified the Demiurge as the Greek God Zeus θευς.

The principle of trinity is found in all the world's religions. 22 Arabic consonants, 22 sacred Hebrew letters, the Ancient Chinese have passed the numbers 1-10 as sacred symbols, within their philosophical set-up of Taoism as Yin and Yang, a male and female representation of Cosmos, Tao (Yin and Yang combined) the same one found in Ancient Egypt as Female and Male consciousness manifestation, or in Hinduism of Kundalini (7 chakras *3 gunas) representation.

Going back many thousands of years, we find that some of our wise ancestors mastered the magic of sound and its frequencies, creating extra-ordinary art using the sacred symbols, expressing cosmic, universal, conscious and sub consciousness concepts giving us a possibility to experience the metaphysics of the philosophy of their time.

It is a symbolic representation of primordial forces that materialize in magical, mysterious fashion while obeying precise universal laws.

Daleth Kabbalah number three 3 is represented by The Empress. It is Daleth = Door governed by Venus. The Formula of the Universe is Love. Venus combines the highest spiritual with the lowest material qualities. Within Alchemy She represents Salt. Salt is the inactive principle of

Nature. It is the Gate of Heaven.

Tree of Life Tarot and Symbolism of Number 3

The Tarot cards with number three refer to Binah that symbolises Understanding. The idea is represented by a triangle that symbolises stability. The stability of wands (fire) manifests itself as Virtues. The three of cups (water) manifests as Abundance. The three of swords (air) emphasise the energy of division within the Sorrow and the three of pentacles (earth) crystallises as: Work.

Egypt and Number 3

In Egypt: 3 three is the number of plurality. Re, Isis, and Anubis, three Gods representing a closed unified system which is complete and interactive among its parts. There are many triads of deities symbolising this triangle of forces: Amun, Re, and Ptah or Osiris, Isis and Horus in its father, mother and son relationship. In some Egyptian triads the

Egyptian king took the role of the divine son. The Egyptian year was divided into three seasons, and each of the twelve months was divided into three ten-days periods.

Egyptian Anch Symbol

Michael Grech, in his article in Malta Times: The Not So Maltese Cross, How the emblem of debauched foreign aristocracy became the ultimate symbol of Maltese identity, in his chapter Re-inventing a Past, reflects the sentiment of our grand-fathers: "Most likely, the cross was gradually and widely adopted by the local population as a national symbol in the 19th century, during the British occupation of islands, when an artificial history about our past was being concocted in response to the new political and cultural situation. Politically and culturally sensitive Maltese wanted to detach themselves from their Southern and Eastern neighbors not merely religiously, but ever more culturally and ethnically." "Colonialism as such was not questioned. The islands' links to Europe were emphasized, exaggerated and at times invented. A greater proximity than in reality existed between the locals and the Order of Saint John was imagined.

The siege of 1565 became THE EVENT. The adoption of the Order's cross as a symbol of local identity fitted neatly into this program. The Maltese Cross was meant to allude to hagiographic and mythological pictures of past greatness; the valiant Knights of St John and their Maltese allies heroically defending 'Christianity' or 'European civilization' from Muslims, Ottomans and non-European others. The hagiography in question and the use of the Maltese cross indicated the past greatness which Maltese wanted to emulate..."

The above paragraph just perfectly resonates of how complex our historical conditions are, and how complicated our sense of identity could possible become, especially if we came from the countries that have in the past defended Pythagoras, Plato, or Neo-Platonic Philosophical Truths.

Ankh or ANX is one of the most recognizable symbols from ancient Egypt, known as "cross of life", dating from 3,000 BC. The symbol is an Egyptian hieroglyph for "life" or "breath of life" = nh = ankh = nX Tracing the sound back in time, we come across X, that was used by the Kings and Priestesses of the Ancient Egyptian New Kingdom. It is carried by the ancient Egyptian gods, goddesses in tomb paintings and worn by Egyptians as an amulet, a golden cross if you wish, around the neck. Ankh, loved and despised by many, have you ever wondered why... An ancient Egyptian symbol often drawn by our wise ancestors was the symbol used by priests and priestesses to represent resurrection and the Holy Spirit.

A crux ansata as a symbol of the Egyptian Anx and resurrection in Codex Glazier a Coptic manuscript New Testament 400 AC

Often interpreted as the word for "life", it traveled across the seas to many ancient civilizations and as the sign was used in the artwork of the Minoan civilization in Crete (Ancient Greece). Even the writing that Minoans used resembles ancient Egyptian hieroglyphs. The ankh continued to be used after the Christianization of Egypt during the 400 AD. The sign was used by early Christians as a monogram for Jesus.

China and Number 3

The number 3 三 sān represents heavens, earth and mankind. It is considered a lucky number. The character sounds similar to the character for 'birth'.

Spiritual Meaning of Number (4) Four

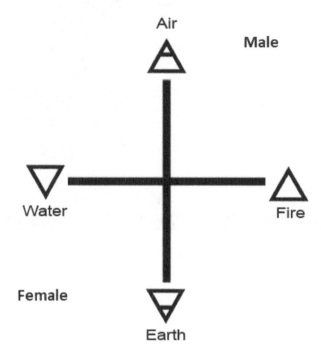

Air

Male

Water

Fire

Female

Earth

Within the Hebrew Kabbalah Symbolism Four 4 is represented by the Tarot card called: The Emperor. The letter associated with it is Tzaddi = Head. The astrological sign is Aries ruled by Mars. Alchemical symbol of Sulphur, male fiery energy of the Universe.

The Crowley Tarot Card 4 symbolises the Initiative of all Being. Hindu call it: Rajas. The four is symbolically 'below the Abyss' within the Tree of Life, so it means solidification.

In the Wand suit (fire) we get Completion. The four of cups (water) is called Luxury. The four of Swords (air) is called Truce. The four of disks (earth) manifest Power.

Egypt Symbolic Meaning of the Number 4

In Egypt this is the number of totality and completeness. We see: four sides of pyramids, the four sons of Horus, four magical bricks, four pillars of the sky, four elder spirits, four cardinal points (directions: north, south, east, west). The ritual of the king's coronation used the four directions: four arrows were shot to the four cardinal points and four birds released. The symbolic use of the number four is frequently the one of completeness, the completeness of a square.

China Symbolic Meaning of Number 4

The Number 4 四 sì is considered an unlucky number because it sounds as the word 'death' in Hong Kong it is common that the 4th floor within a building just does not exist.

Jung and Number 4

"The symbolic structures that seem to refer to the process of individuation tend to be based on the motif of the number four such as the four functions of consciousness, or the four stages of the anima or animus."

Man and His Symbols by Carl Jung

FIRE.

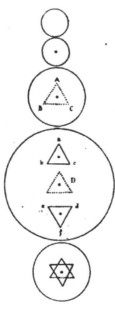

The Universal Principle.

The Boundless Power.
The Universal Root.

He who has stood, stands,
and will stand.

The Middle Distance,
Incomprehensible Air,
Without beginning or end,
Generated by
The Spirit (The Seventh
Power) moving on the
Waters.

The Lower Regions or World
made by the Angels and

The Perfect Intellectual.

Invisible, Inapprehensible
Silence.

A. Incorruptible Form.
B. Universal Mind.
C. Great Thought.

a. Mind (Heaven).
b. Voice (Sun).
c. Reason (Air).
D. The Image from the
Incorruptible Form,
alone ordering all
things.
d. Reflection (Water).
e. Name (Moon).
f. Thought (Earth).

Powers, who were generated
by Thought.[1]

Diagram of the Simonian Aeonology Mind — Thought Heaven — Earth
Voice — Name Sun — Moon Reason — Desire Air — Water

Spiritual Meaning of Number (5) Five

Vau Hebrew letter symbolic meaning of number 5. 5 is represented by the Hierophant. The letter Vau = a Nail. Astrologically ruled by Taurus that is Earth in its strongest and most balanced form.

Crowley Tarot Card Five shows the idea of motion that is not balanced.

The five of Wands (fire) is called Strife.

The five of cups (water) is called Disappointment.

The five Swards (air) symbolises Defeat.

The five of disks (earth) is called Worry.

Chinese Symbolism of Number 5

The number 5 五 wǔ is associated with the five Chinese elements: Water, Fire, Earth, Wood, and Metal. It is a strong number combining the energies of 2 and 3. However it is associated with the word 'not' and some consider it unbalanced and unlucky.

Spiritual Meaning of Number 6: Lucky or Unlucky?

Kabbalah Tarot and Number 6

Hebrew letter six 6 is represented by the Lovers ruled by Mercury, sign of Gemini. Letter Zain = Sword. Symbolising Analysis and Synthesis.

The number six within the Tree of Life is attributed to Tiphareth.

Tiphareth is at the centre of the Tree of Life. It is the only Sephira that communicates directly with Kether. It is balanced horizontally and vertically symbolically representing a cross.

It symbolises the Sun. It represents consciousness in its harmony.

The number six represents the energy of the elements at its best manifestation. The six of Wands (fire) is called Victory. The six of Cups (water) is called Pleasure. The six of Swards (air) is called Science and the six of Disks (earth) is called Success.

China and Meaning of Number 6

6 六 liù in Mandarin is pronounced similar to 'flow' and is considered good for business, it represents wealth, six also represents longevity, expansiveness and celestial powers.

Magic Number 6

'Its number is 6. It refers therefore, to the dual nature of the Logos as divine and human; the interlacing of the upright and averse triangles in the hexagram. It is the first number of the Sun, whose last number is 666, "the number of a man".'

Crowley about magic of number six

Magic of Number 7

7 is often chosen as the 'luckiest' number. A resent poll of 30,000 people in the US confirmed that 7 is the favourite number followed by 3.

"Seven is the number of perfection. Observation of man himself will make this clear. Today he is under the influence of the number five insofar as he can be good or evil. As a creature of the universe he lives in the number four. When he will have developed all that he holds at present as germ within him, he will become a seven-membered being, perfect in its kind. The number seven rules in the world of colour, in the rainbow; in the world of tone it is found in the scale. Everywhere, in all realms of life, the number seven can be observed as a kind of number of perfection. There is no superstition or magic in this."

Rudolf Steiner about meaning of numbers, Occult Symbols and Signs

Kabbalah and Number Seven 7

7 is represented by the Chariot, Letter Chet, Ruled by Cancer that is the cardinal sign of the water element.

The number seven is attributed to Netzach within the Kabbalah's Tree of Life. Their position is unbalanced and they bring forth the degeneration of the element.

The seven of Wands (fire) is called Valour and it represents Mars with its worst energies. The seven of cups (water) degenerates into addictions, madness, false pleasure where Venus goes against Venus. The seven of Swards (air) is called Futility. The seven of Disks (earth) is called Failure.

Egypt and Number 7

In Egypt the number seven carried within the concept of perfection and effectiveness. It is 3 and 4 combined and it carries the qualities of completeness and self-sufficiency. The number seven is of a great importance in Egyptian magic: seven scorpions escort the Goddess Isis to provide her with maximum magic protection. It is seven days that Nut carries her child within her womb.

China and Lucky Number 7

In China the number 7七qī symbolizes togetherness. It is a lucky number for relationships. The character sounds like the Chinese word qì meaning 'life essence'. Many ceremonies in China are celebrated on the seventh day to acknowledge seven as the number of a perfectly completed cycle.

Spiritual Meaning of Number 8

Kabbalah Tarot and Meaning of Number 8

Meaning of number eight, Tarot, letter tet tree of life 8 is represented by the Tarot card called Justice, letter Tet. The sign is Libra, representing Balance, the cardinal sign of the element Air.

It symbolises Karma and it is manifested within 'Love is the law, love under will'.

The eight of Wands (fire) is called Swiftness. Fire no longer has the element of destruction.

The eight of Cups (water) is called Indolence. Sorrow rules the water element bringing in internal and external stress.

The eight of Swards (air) is called Interference or unforeseen bad luck.

The eight of Disks (earth) is called Prudence or 'put some money away for the rainy days'.

Chinese Lucky Number Eight

The word for 8/\ bā sounds similar to the word which means 'prosper' or 'wealth''

The number 8 is viewed as so auspicious that a number with several eights is considered very lucky.

In 2003, A telephone number with all digits being eights was sold for $280,000.

The opening ceremony of the Olympics in China began on 8/8/08 at 8:08:08 PM

Eight is an important number in Buddhism. The Eight-fold-Noble-Path is given by Buddha as an instruction towards enlightenment. Eight is found on many religious symbols surrounding Buddha.

Divine Meaning of Number 9

Use of Nomina Sacra expressing divine

Tree of Life, Tarot, Number 9

9 is represented by the Hermit. Yod = the Hand, symbolizes the Father, Wisdom, the Logos, the Creator, Mercury

Zoroaster says: 'the number Nine is sacred, and attains the summit of perfection.'

Jung about number 9:

"The nine has been a "magic number" for centuries. According to the traditional symbolism of numbers, it represents the perfect form of the perfected Trinity in its threefold elevation."

The nine of Wands is called Strength.

The nine of Cups is called Happiness.

The nine of Swards is called Cruelty. The original disruption is raised to its highest power.

The nine of Disks is called Gain. The earth becomes more and more solid.

Egypt and Divine Nine

Egyptians see nine as the number three multiplied by itself, a great number that multiplies the qualities of the number three.

China Meaning of Nine

In China the number 9 九 jiŭ was associated with the Emperor. The Emperor's robes often had nine dragons, and the dragon had nine children. This number symbolizes divine harmony.

The number 9 is the same as the word for 'long lasting' so it is often used in weddings.

Spiritual Meaning of Number 10

Tree of Life and Meaning of Number 10

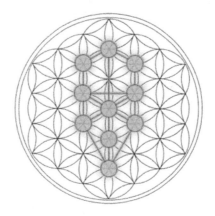

10 is represented by the Tarot Card called Fortune. The letter is Kaph = the palm of the hand. Ruled by Jupiter, the Great Fortune planet, manifesting Universe with its 3 forms of manifestation: rajas, tamas, sattvas.

The ten of Wands (fire) is called Oppression. The constant use of force kills the energy manifestation. The ten of Cups (water) is called Satiety. The ten of Swords (air) is called Ruin. The ten of Disks (earth) is called Wealth.

Egypt and Number 10

In Egypt this number was connected with the measurement of time and space.

Light and Divine

Like bees and butterflies around a candle light during a dark night, our bodies, minds and souls get attracted to the 'light'. The symbolism of Light around the world is mapped within our spiritual practices that use 'Light' as a medium and our spiritual experiences of Divine that often have 'light' as the central point.

We use words like: 'divine light', 'clear light', 'enlightenment', 'pure light', 'light body', 'astral light' to express our highest meditative states, prayer contemplations, and our overall connection with what we call 'Divine'.

Symbolism of Light

Even though we see God as encompassing, omnipotent and omnipresent, we prefer to meet Him or Her diving into the qualities of 'light' rather than 'darkness'. Light attracts our souls' imagination and our symbolic spiritual journey is the one of: 'lightness of being', 'light carriers', 'light diamond body'.

The symbolism of 'light' all across the cultures connects us with consciousness, wisdom, moral purity, intelligence, angels, beauty.

Light and Various Religious Practices

The worship of light in the form of sun worship or fire worship is one of the earliest form of worships.

The Hebrew saw the very beginning of creation as: 'God said: Let there be light, and there was light'

Zoroaster, in ancient Persia, called the principle of light, Ormuzd that was born of the purest light and the principle of darkness, Ahriman that sprung from utter darkness.

Pythagoras also believed that two antagonistic principles rule the creation. The first one was unity, light, the right hand, stability, symbolised by a straight line; the second one was darkness, the left hand, instability, symbolised by a curved line.

The Cabalists say that before the creation of the world, existed only Aur en soph, or the Eternal Light, and when the Divine Mind willed to become Nature, the Eternal Light emanated its radiance from a central point.

Inner Light

It is the inner light that comes forth from complete darkness, from silence of meditation and contemplation that is the true light of wisdom.

Spiritual Quotes About Light as Divine Force

The Symbolism of Freemasonry, by Albert G. Mackey, 1882, The Masonic Rite of Intrusting

'It (This rite of intrusting) begins, however, with the communication of LIGHT, which, although but a preparation for the development of the mysteries which are to follow, must be considered as one of the most important symbols in the whole science of masonic symbolism. So important, indeed, is it, and so much does it pervade with its influence and its relations the whole masonic system, that Freemasonry itself anciently received, among other appellations, that of Lux, or Light, to signify that it is to be regarded as that sublime doctrine of Divine Truth by which the path of him who has attained it is to be illuminated in his pilgrimage of life.'

Rudolf Steiner Spiritual Poem about Light and Archangel Michael, the ruler of Cosmic Intelligence

The importance of Light within the Taoist Spiritual Practice

The Chi Kung exercises are based upon the circulation of the imaginary Light through the different energy centres. According to Taoists, Light cleanses and gives the practitioner an amazing source of Strength.

'The Golden Flower is the Light. What colour has the light? One uses the Golden Flower as an image. It is the true power of the transcendent Great One...'

Light and Sun-Gazing

Some ancient spiritual practices use sun-gazing to feed neurons and cells within the body transforming this light into nourishment. Sun gazing is often practiced with the bare feet on the earth. Safe hours for sun-gazing are half an hour after sunrise and half an hour before sunset. Manek, 69, from India, claims that since 1995 he has lived only on sun-gazing and water.

Light and our addiction to Screens

All our 'screens' radiate light. TV, computer, mobile screens, all first communicate with our eyes through the light.

Our fascination with 'light' could be one of the sub-conscious reasons to our addiction to screens.

Gratefully Giving & Receiving Divine Flow

Now imagine White Light, by Nuit from Art of 4 Elements

'Light waves are waves of energy in the form of electric and magnetic fields. The amount of energy in a light wave is proportional to its frequency: high frequency light has high energy; low frequency light has low energy. The frequency of visible light is: colour, and ranges from low frequency red, to high frequency violet. The combination of every colour in the visible spectrum produces white. The full range of frequencies extends beyond the visible spectrum, so we have radio waves, ultra violet rays, etc. Light waves move at their maximum 300,000 kilometres per second which makes light the fastest phenomenon in the universe...'

by Nuit from Art of 4 Elements Book

4 Elements Wedding Ceremony

This Wedding Ritual was inspired and created for a dear friend's wedding and it is here to inspire you to create your-own ritual respecting the blessings of 4 elements and the Mother Earth.

Blessings to the Couple

"We gathered here to acknowledge and deepen the soul-mate union of these two lovely souls. We are here to support this amazing Twin Flame honouring the Bounty of Life.

May you take steps in trust holding each other through all of your vulnerabilities and learnings, co-creating Life together, opening deeper towards Love, Love that is Wild, Love that is Still.

May Angels give you Wisdom to cherish, nurture, and respect one another, choosing trust and honesty above All.

May God give you Strength to resonate with the Song of Life fully honouring the truth of each other.

Mother of Form and the Father of Consciousness Unite within this Sacred Marriage!"

4 Elements Wedding Ritual

Prepare a table with four elements (symbols) placed on it respecting the 4 Directions.

Air = East = Yellow = Rising Sun = Birth

In its highest manifestation Air is symbolised by an Eagle (if you have an Eagle feather use it within the ritual). The air is purified with an incense (a wonderful one is Nag Champa), and you offer your respect to the stage of Birth, asking Sages and Saints to support the Birth of Good and Fruitful Initiatives. A flute creates a magic of sound. The incense is passed around participants.

Fire = South = Red = Life Force Manifestations

Candles are lit, the couple is holding them. Fire in its highest manifestation is Divine Love. Represented by a Lion. The candles are given around to people to hold. We ask Angels to guide our Life Force towards Divine Love.

Water = West = Dark Blue = Emotions = Setting Sun

The couple is holding two vessels with water. They mix the water pouring it from one vessel into the other. You mix into the water some essential oils (good ones representing the element of water are: Jasmine, Rose, Lavender. Pass the vessels around. Water in its highest manifestation is Peace. Dragon is the Symbol of Water's Highest Manifestation. We ask Ancestors to guide us towards Peace.

Earth = North = white = winter = Wisdom of Elders

You have two vessels with sand and you mix them together pouring the sand from one vessel to the other. The elephant represents the eternal strength and a capability to overcome any obstacle.

The highest manifestation of Earth energies is the Land of Plenty. We ask Scientists to help us live within the World of Plenty.

The Central Force

The central force, the force that unites all the elements is Tao, Life Force, the Mother Earth, represented by Green. A green branch is passed along to symbolise Life.

The Tree of Life is the symbol of this Life Force. Passing the branch you say the vows to each other. Passing the branch, the people around say their blessings.

We all say: "Mother of Form and the Father of Consciousness Unite within this Sacred Marriage." The couple kisses, the participants surround them within an Universal Hug, and all participants sing AUM or a chosen sacred song.

4 Elements Ritual Wedding Poem by Nuit

Finding the words to describe this magic ceremony that happened at the Equinox, this poem came to me...
Taking steps in trust, child-full playfulness and joyful peace
Chanting, drumming, humming, dancing at the most Sacred Palace
Resonating with the Song of Life
We touched the Spiral where Forest meets Rivers
Ascending the deepest caves where Stalactites and Stalagmites form Castles
Of Eternal Lovers meditating within the Earth's Belly
Mirroring What is Below is Above
We were 12 Honourable Guests witnessing the Sacred Marriage
The Mother of Form united with the Father of Consciousness
Asking Sages, Saints to give our Initiatives Fruitfulness
Angels to protect our Fire of Life
Ancestors to guard our Wisdom
Scientists to guide us towards the Land of Plenty
Holding each other's space, souls' expression, laughter
We honoured the 4 elements letting the Equinox
Flow through the Spiral of our DNAs
Worshiping the Central Force that unites us with the Universe
Becoming a Vessel of Love that is Life
We merged with Tao.

Meditation Spiritual and Occult Symbols

During the spiritual training a meditator can use visual images, mantras or words, or feelings and sensations (such as compassion, love, peace) as a focus of a meditation.

Thousands of years of spiritual practice short-listed a number of sacred occult symbols of meditation that affect the soul in a special way when it withdraws all attention from the outer world, and focusses on an image, mantra or a feeling.

How to Meditate on Symbols

During the Meditation on Symbols, one focus on a symbol allowing different ideas and impressions into the mind. This is the way to contemplate the symbol.

During the meditation, helped by Rhythmical Breathing, we silence the mind and allow our soul to become one with the symbol within the silence. The symbol will inspire our Soul to enter deeper meditations.

Meditation Symbols in Buddhism

Buddha Eyes or Wisdom Eyes

Buddha Eyes look at us from all the Tibetan Stupas in Nepal gazing in the four directions to symbolize the all-knowing Buddha.

Between the Buddha's eyes there is the Nepali character for the number 1, symbolizing unity of all things and the Buddha's all-seeing third eye.

According to Buddhism all beings have the Buddha nature. We all have within us the seed of purity that is to be transformed and developed into Buddhahood.

Dharma Wheel

The Eight Spoked Dharma Wheel in Sanskrit called: 'Dharmachakra' symbolises the Buddha's Wheel of Karma. Eight spokes symbolise the Eight-fold-Noble-Path that is given by Buddha as an instruction towards enlightenment. The 3 symbols in the centre represent 3 jewels or the pillars: the Buddha, the Dharma: his teachings and the Sangha: spiritual community

The Buddha is known as the Wheel-Turner: the One who sets a new cycle of life in motion and changes the destiny.

Meditation on Buddha

Meditating on the image of Buddha or repeating mantras, the ordinary body, speech and mind are purified and transformed into Buddha's holy body, holy speech and holy mind.

Hindu Meditations and Yantras

Sri Yantra

Shree Yantra is considered to be the Queen of all Yantras. Its shape is composed of 9 triangles mystically drawn one within the other on the inside of the mandala. It shows how this basic mathematical pattern governs the evolution of life. The Sri Yantra is believed to be the image of the OM mantra, according to Hindus: the primordial sound of creation.

Yantras are used for inner healing, and meditation. Coming from India and Tibet, since 3000 B.C. yantras have powerful symbolic messages for our subconscious worlds. Every shape emits a very specific energy pattern and a person who meditates on a yantra tunes into this specific frequency.

The Sri Yantra in the 3 dimensional shape (Meru in Sanskrit) is a Pyramid grid signifying unlimited Universe and its abundance. Meaning of Shree is 'Wealth'.

'Meditation means properly the concentration of the mind on a single train of ideas which work out a single subject. Contemplation means regarding mentally a single object, image, idea so that the knowledge about the object, image or idea may arise naturally in the mind by force of the concentration.'

'This form leads to another, the emptying of all thought out of the mind so as to leave it a sort of pure vigilant blank on which the divine knowledge may come and imprint itself, undisturbed by the inferior thoughts of the ordinary human mind and with the clearness of a writing in white chalk on a blackboard... This may be called the dhyana of liberation, as it frees the mind from slavery to the mechanical process of thinking and allows it to think or not to think, as it pleases and when it pleases, or to choose its own thoughts or else to go beyond thought to the pure perception of Truth called in our philosophy Vijnana.'

Sri Aurobindo Meditation Quotes

Meditation on Shiva

Lord Śiva (Shiva), the Destroyer or the Transformer is one of the three major Gods in Hinduism; he is part of the Trimurti (three forms) that is the Hindu Trinity, that explains that the cosmic energies manifest in three forms: creation, maintenance, and destruction, and they are personified as Bramha, Vishnu and Shiva.

It is Siva who causes bondage and who made Maya (Illusion). It is Siva who makes you realise your essential Divine Nature. Siva created the idea of egoism, Karma, pleasure and pain. It is Siva who offers Moksha or freedom. Om and Siva are one. Siva manifests in the Gayatri Mantra, Agni and in the Sun.

Meditation and Christianity

Meditation is more-or-less defined as a mental exercise of concentration and contemplation, by either focusing on a single thought (e.g. meditation repeating a mantra), or by following an intuitive imaginative flow that involves relaxing the body, and calming the river of thoughts, with an aim to enter deeper levels of consciousness.

St. Teresa of Avila Christian mystic about meditation

For Mystical Christians meditation is a type of contemplative practice often known as prayer, induced by inspirational readings, and practiced with a form of visualization.

In both Eastern traditions and the Christian tradition the goal of contemplative practices is a closer intimacy with God, Christ, Buddha, Shiva consciousness, or a Guru.

The Mystical Christians would completely agree with the Yoga gurus of our present and past about the benefits of meditation.

St. Teresa of Avila (1515-1582)
A Mystic Christian Saint about Prayer

There are 4 stages towards God:
1. Devout **contemplation or concentration**
2. The '**prayer of quiet**' where the prevailing state is one of quietude
3. The '**devotion of union**',
an **ecstatic state of a blissful peace,**
4. The '**devotion of ecstasy**', the **body consciousness disappears**, sense activity ceases; and the body is literally lifted into space.

What is meditation?

Alchemy of Love
Mindfulness Training

St. Teresa of Avila 1515-1582 Christian Mystic about Meditation

St. Teresa of Avila a Christian Saint living during the 16th Century wrote about 4 stages towards God and her inspiring words of contemplation very much resemble the description of a Yogi that talks about meditation. She names the four stages to God as:

1. Contemplation and concentration
2. Prayer of quiet or SILENCE
3. Devotion of UNION or "ecstatic state of blissful peace"
4. Devotion of ECSTASY, where "the body Consciousness disappears".

Meditation as a Spiritual not Religious Tool

We are lucky to be living at times when all the ancient scripts are readily available for us to read, compare, and thoroughly research. All the different cultures across the Globe work with this ancient spiritual practice and its application within the day-to-day life.

Whether we read the Yogic text Patanjali (150-200BC) Yoga Sutras, or the Chinese ancient texts like: The Secret of the Golden Flower (around 600AC) we come across various examinations of meditation as the spiritual tool, researching its relationship with Health, Balance, Mind and Soul. The Hindus, or Buddhists Priests and Yogi practitioners, explore this amazing laboratory of various mystical applications of meditation within their lives and the mystical Christians or Sufi practitioners (Islam) are no exception to this rule.

Using our souls intent, we approach meditation either mentally or through our hearts, and we learn about the whole range of benefits that this practice offers; physical or emotional relaxation, improved concentration, increased love, At the end of the spiritual journey we find the promise of Enlightenment, or eternal Happiness.

Detaching the tool from the religious connotations is always a difficult process and it risks "charlatans" invading the space of Gurus, Philosophers, Sages, Priests, and Spiritual Researchers promising an "instant happiness", a "curse" or a "pink pill" that cure all the diseases and brings immense wealth without any "Proper Rightful Effort", without a rigorous self-development training that truly works with Virtues, Creativity, Changing Habits, etc.

Meditation is today a focus of increasing scientific research and over 1,000 research studies are published linking meditation to a variety of health benefits, stress reduction, improvement of academic performance, sustained attention, increasing the one's self control, and love. From the point of view of psychology, meditation can induce altered states of consciousness.

Difference between Concentration and Meditation

'Concentration and meditation are the royal roads to perfection. Concentration leads to meditation. Fix the mind on one object either within the body or without. Keep it there steadily for some time. This is concentration. You will have to practise this daily. Purify the mind first through the practice of right conduct and then take to the practice of concentration.'

'Concentration purifies and calms the surging emotions, strengthens the current of thought and clarifies the ideas. Concentration helps a man in his material progress also. He will have a very good outturn of work in his office or business house. What was cloudy and hazy before becomes clear and definite.'

'Meditation is of two kinds viz., Saguna Dhyana (concrete meditation) and Nirguna Dhyana (abstract meditation). In concrete meditation the Yogic student meditates on the form of Lord Krishna, Rama, Sita, Vishnu, Siva, Gayatri or Devi. In abstract meditation he meditates on his own Self or Atman.'

Swami Sivananda: Meditation and Concentration with Symbols

Meditation on Symbolism of Mars, Venus, Jupiter, Moon

Following the circle, the Babylonians used the number system based on sixes and modern system of counting hours, seconds and minutes is based on it. The celestial events were viewed by the Babylonians as divine intervention in their lives expressing the influence the sun, moon, and planets, and to communicate when bad or good events were going to occur. The Babylonians were the first people to apply myths to constellations and astrology and describe the 12 signs of the zodiac. These are found as carved in stone tablets.

The oldest cuneiform literature of Babylonians divide the fixed stars into three groups: the stars of Anu, Enlil and Ea.
Of the planets five were recognized: Jupiter, Venus, Saturn, Mercury and Mars. These five planets were identified with the gods of the Babylonian pantheon as: Jupiter as Bel-Marduk, Venus as Ishtar, Saturn as Ninurta, Ninib, Mercury as Nabu. Nebo, Mars as Nergal. The movements of the Sun, Moon and five planets were regarded as representing the activity of the five gods.

The movements of the Sun, Moon and five planets were regarded as representing the activity of the five gods.

Moon

Sīn or Suen (Akkadian: 𒂗𒍪 EN.ZU or lord-ess of wisdom) or Nanna was the number 30, in cuneiform: 𒌍 (10 x 3) the god/goddess of the moon in the Mesopotamian religions of Sumer, Akkad, Assyria and Babylonia. Nanna (the classical Sumerian spelling is DŠEŠ.KI = the technical term for the crescent moon, also refers to the deity, is a Sumerian deity worshiped in Ur (Syria you must have guessed).

Selene, or Latin Luna, was the personification of the moon as a goddess. She was worshipped at the new and full moons. Many languages have beautiful words for Moon. It is "Luna" in Italian, Latin and Spanish, "Lune" in French, "Mesec" in Slavic, "Mond" in German. Slavic and Germanic countries have the Moon as the male gender. In Babylon SiN was also of a male gender. In Slavic "SiN" means "Son". Luna commonly refers to: Earth's moon, named "Luna" in Latin; Luna (goddess), the ancient Roman personification of the Moon.

The ancient sages respected the wisdom of the Moon and its phases. The ancient Chinese called the Sun Tai Yang, or the Great Yang Luminary. They called the Moon Tai Yin, or the Great Yin Luminary. In Hinduism, the Sun is Shiva, while the Moon is Shakti, God and Goddess. Shiva is consciousness, while Shakti is the Soul in its manifestation on Earth.

Sīn or Akkadian: □□ EN.ZU or Nanna (Sumerian: □□□ DŠEŠ.KI) was the god of the moon in the Mesopotamian religions of Sumer, Akkad, Assyria and Babylonia.

Ishtar

Ishtar, in Mesopotamian religion, goddess of sexual love. Ishtar's primary legacy from the Sumerian tradition is the role of fertility figure. Ishtar cult center was Uruk as early as 4,000 BC. Her influence extend to modern-day Iraq, Kuwait and parts of Syria, Iran, and Turkey including the Akkadian, Babylonian and Assyrian Empires.

1900 BC - 1600 BC the poem "Descent of Inanna" is written, ritualized, worshipped. Inanna is Ishtar in Sumerian sources.

This powerful Mesopotamian goddess is the first known deity for which rituals were written. The skill of writing is closely related to this period. Later liturgies of all the religions copy the style and ritual recorded on the stone tablets - the call and response, the alphabet as sacred symbols, music and religious poetry to god / gods.

Venus as the Goddess of Love.

In Greek mythology, Persephone (pər-SEF-ə-nee; Greek: Περσεφόνη), also called Kore (KOR-ee; Greek: Κόρη; "the maiden"), is the daughter of Zeus and Demeter. She became the queen of the underworld through her abduction by Hades, the god of the underworld.

Persephone as a vegetation goddess and her mother Demeter were the central figures of the Eleusinian Mysteries, which promised the initiated happiness after death. In some versions, Persephone is the mother of Zeus' son Dionysus, (or Iacchus, and/or Zagreus) an ancient cult of agricultural communities.

In Classical Greek art, Persephone is portrayed robed, carrying a sheaf of grain. She is identified by the Romans as Libera or Libra (VaGa in Slavic).

Jupiter

Jupiter (Latin: Iuppiter) is the king of the gods in Roman mythology. He is known as Zeus θεuς in Greek mythology. Both Greek Zeus and Roman God Iovis ['jɔwɪs]) also known as JoVe – were represented as Jupiter, the Main God. Belos was recognized in Babylonian astrology as the planet Jupiter.

Steiner's Meditation upon Rose and Cross

'In my thoughts I look now, for example, upon the rose and say, In the red rose petal I see the colour of the green plant sap transformed into red, and the red rose, like the green leaf, follows the pure, passionless laws of growth. The red of the rose may now become the symbol of a blood that is the expression of purified instincts and passions that have stripped off all that is base, and in their purity resemble the forces active in the red rose. I now seek not merely to imbue my intellect with such thoughts but to bring them to life in my feelings. I may have a feeling of bliss when I think of the purity and passionless of the growing plant; I can produce within myself the feeling of how certain higher perfections must be purchased through the acquirement of instincts and desires. This can then transform the feeling of bliss, which I have felt previously, into a grave feeling; and then a feeling of liberating joy may stir in me when I surrender myself to the thought of the red blood which, like the red sap of the rose, may become the bearer of inwardly pure experiences."

"It is of importance that we do not without feeling confront the thoughts that serve to construct such a symbolic visualization. After we have pondered on such thoughts and feelings for a time, we are to transform them into the following symbolic visualization. We visualize a black cross. Let this be the symbol of the destroyed base elements of instincts and passions, and at the centre, where the arms of the cross intersect, let us visualize seven red, radiant roses arranged in a circle. Let these roses be the symbol of a blood that is the expression of purified, cleansed passions and instincts.'

Rudolf Steiner Meditation: Symbol of Cross and Rose, Occult Science

Oberon Titania and Puck with Fairies Dancing By William Blake 1786 Tate Museum the UK

The Meaning of Om

The mantra OM is the name of God. Written as A-U-M, it represents the divine energy united in its three aspects: Brahma (creation), Vishnu (preservation) and Shiva (destruction); or Buddhists will relate it to holy body, holy speech and holy mind of Buddha.

Swami Sivananda about the Meaning of Om and Om Meditation

'Om (Aum) is everything. Om is the Name or symbol of God, Isvara or Brahman. Om is your real Name. Om covers the whole threefold experience of man. Om stands for the phenomenal worlds. From Om this sense-universe has been projected. The world exists in Om and dissolves in Om. 'A' represents the physical plane. 'U' represents the mental and astral plane, the world of intelligent spirits, all heavens. 'M' represents the whole deep sleep state, and all that is unknown even in your wakeful state, all that is beyond the reach of your intellect. Om represents all, Om is the basis of your life, thought and intelligence. Om is everything. All words which denote objects are centred in Om. Hence the whole world has come from Om, rests in Om, and dissolves in Om. As soon as you sit for meditation, chant Om loudly 3 or 6 or 12 times. This will drive away all worldly thoughts from the mind and remove Vikshepa (tossing of mind). Then take to the mental repetition of Om.

The Japa of Om (Pranava Japa) has a tremendous influence on the mind... The vibrations set up by this word are so powerful that, if one persists in taking recourse to them, they would bring the largest building to the ground... Pronounced as spelt, it will have a certain effect upon the student; but pronounced in its correct method, it arouses and transforms every atom in his physical body, setting up new vibrations and conditions, and awakening the sleeping power of the body.'

Spiritual Messages from Enlightened Minds

'As a mother would risk her life to protect her child, her only child, even so should one cultivate a limitless heart with regard to all beings. So with a boundless heart should one cherish all living beings; radiating kindness over the entire world.'

The Buddha, About Compassion, Sutta Nipata I, 8

Lao Tzu, Tao Te Ching, Chapter 2

'When the world knows beauty as beauty, ugliness arises
When it knows good as good, evil arises
Thus being and non-being produce each other
Difficult and easy bring about each other
Long and short reveal each other
High and low support each other
Music and voice harmonize each other
Front and back follow each other
Therefore the sages:
Manage the work of detached actions
Conduct the teaching of no words
They work with myriad things but do not control
They create but do not possess
They act but do not presume
They succeed but do not dwell on success
It is because they do not dwell on success
That it never goes away'
Bible, Mark, 12:30-31

'and you shall love the Lord your God with all your heart, with all your soul, with all your mind, and with all your strength.' The second is this, 'YOU SHALL LOVE YOUR NEIGHBOR AS YOURSELF.' There is no other commandment greater than these.'

Magic and Meaning of Equinox

The seasons change while the Earth continues its journey through the space and time. Rituals at the Spring and Autumn Equinox honour balance between light and dark.

Some teachings of esoteric wisdom say that during this time the veil between the physical world and other worlds opens. This is a good time for meditation, prayers, rituals and offerings.

Autumn Equinox

The autumn equinox is a time of death, the time to destroy the egos and our subconscious patterns such as anger, pride, greed, envy, lust... We can offer our weaknesses as sacrifices before the gods transforming them into their higher, divine manifestation.

Chinese honour this time with a ritual of standing facing west, lighting white candles, or placing white flowers on the altar.

The Druids used to cut wands from the willow trees to use for divination at this time of year.

For the ancient Celts the autumn equinox is symbolically marked as a time of sacrifice with a ritual of burning a figure from the stems of grain, representing the vegetation spirit.

Rituals at Equinox

The Equinox is also known as: Cornucopia, Feast of Avilon, Festival of Dionysus, Mabon, Night of the Hunter, Witch's Thanksgiving.

There are hundreds of ancient sites all over the world that align to the solstices and equinoxes giving us various mathematical, astronomical, and sacred guidelines.

Equinox in Malta

Mnajdra's (around 4000 BC) Lower Temple

Mnajdra is a megalithic temple complex in Malta, an architectural masterpiece, dating back to 3600 BC.

Its entrance is aligned with the sun rays of the equinox. The rays of light penetrate a corridor and illuminate a back-stone / shrine within the temple. Sunrise on the first day of spring and autumn, during the equinoxes, marks the relationship between the temples and celestial bodies.

Equinox in Egypt

The Great Pyramid

The Great Pyramid has two of its faces orientated precisely towards East and West, meaning that these are the exact points of the rising and setting sun only on the spring and autumnal equinoxes. This kiss of sunlight and sides of the Great Pyramid has probably resulted in a flash of light that was visible for miles around.

At midnight on the autumn equinox North Star shines its light all the way down to the subterranean pit inside the pyramid. In 2,170 BC, the pole star was Alpha Draconis. It is calculated that at the same time in 2,170 BC, Alcyone, the star Mayan believed our sun and solar system revolves around, stood on the meridian of the Great Pyramid.

Equinox in Ireland

Loughcrew built around 3000 B.C. also captures a ray of sunlight through its central chamber exactly on the winter solstice. During the mornings of the equinoxes, the shrine within the temple that is decorated with astronomical symbols, is illuminated by the sun.

Equinox of Mayas

Chichen Itza

Mayas built their sacred site called Chichen Itza with a pyramid known as El Castillo that at spring and autumn equinoxes creates a pattern of light on its nine steps. The game of shadow and light displays seven triangles that link up with a stone serpent head at the base of the pyramid. During the autumn equinox, the setting sun's moving pattern appears to be a snake descending down the steps. The visual effect is the one of the serpent ascending and descending. The feathered serpent is an esoteric symbol of union of female and male aspect. The serpent symbolizes the feminine aspect, and the feathers, the eagle, the male aspect. The ascent and descent of the serpent is the symbolic representation of the descent into the underworld and ascent towards heavens.

Equinox in ancient Sumer

the goddess Inanna, and in Greek mythology the goddess Persephone descend into the underworld at the time of the autumn equinox. Astrologically speaking, this is the day when the Sun enters Libra, the sign of balance. Esoterically, the number 8 that is the symbol of infinity hides within the centre of the earth.

8 is also a symbol of the equinox.

Full Moon Rituals from Around the World

Moon Goddess and Full Moon Rituals

We all know that the Moon has a profound influence upon us. Many say that the highest energy occurs at the Full Moon.

Have you had a chance to meditate, absorb its beauty and its energy? Have you had a chance to pay your respect?

Fool Moon and Astrology

Astrologically the Moon is the closest planet that influences waters on Earth. In a natal chart, Sun represents the conscious will; the personality; and the self-actualization, while the Moon represents the subconscious mind and the feelings and instincts. The moon also transits through one of the 12 constellations. It I either in Leo, or in Virgo, or in Libra, so it gives us specific energies influenced by the stars constellations.

Aries - Action: leadership, authority, rebirth, spiritual conversion, or willpower

Taurus – Sensuality: for physical love, material acquisitions, and money.

Gemini – Communication: good communication, change of residence, writing, public relations, & travel

Cancer – Nurturing: home and domestic life

Leo – Vitality: courage, fertility, or childbirth

Virgo – Organizing: employment, intellectual matters, health

Libra – Balance: artistic work, justice, court cases, partnerships

Scorpio – Philosophical: sex, power, psychic growth, secrets

Capricorn - Ambitious: recognition, career

Aquarius – Social: science, freedom, creative expression

Pisces – Sensitivity: dream work, clairvoyance, telepathy, music

Full Moon and Worship of Divine Mother

The Full Moon is an auspicious time to pay respect to the Divine Mother, to the Shakti.

The new moon energy gives one the power of new beginnings, the full moon (48 hour window) is the best for expressing gratitude, for meditation and prayer.

Full Moon and Buddhism

To Buddhists, there is a special meaning to a full moon day. Buddha was born, got enlightened and died on a full moon day.

Full Moon and 4 Elements

Ancient belief is that the moon is the controller of water.

Fire and Water are the elements of Sun and Moon, where Fire gives light, heat and energy, allowing Water the absorbs light to produce Life.

People suffering from mental dis-easies have their fears and passions affected during full moon days, this is where 'lunatic' word comes from.

Farmers studied the influence of the moon on their crops. Medical science examined the relationship of the moon on human beings observing how the 70% of water in our body reacts modifying our metabolism, electrical charges and blood acidity.

Full Moon Spiritual Practices

The ancient sages respect the wisdom of the Moon and its phases.

Taoist sexual practices suggest that a person avoids sexual merge on quarter or full moons and on days when there were great winds, or storms.

Chinese employ a lunar based calendar. For them Yang is Sun, a Masculine principle within the Nature and Yin is feminine, the Moon or Goddess of the Night.

The ancient Chinese called the Sun Tai Yang, or the Great Yang Luminary. They called the Moon Tai Yin, or the Great Yin Luminary.

In Hinduism, the Sun is Shiva, while the Moon is Shakti, God and Goddess. Shiva is consciousness, while Shakti is the Soul in its manifestation on Earth.

Shamanic Moon Ceremonies

The Most Shamanic rituals honour the spirit of the natural world. The full moon is worshiped with rituals involving burning sage, purification, chanting, dancing and meditation. One of the ceremonies is called 'Drawing Down the Moon' where the energy of the Full Moon is used to induce the trance state of meditation and higher consciousness.

Schumann Resonance

Earth Breathing and Alpha Brainwaves

The earth is surrounded by air, and the ionosphere, and it is a wonderfully resonant system. Any energy trapped within this earth-ionosphere cavity, like lightning storms, etc., will cause it to ring like a bell. This frequency was first time calculated and detected by the German physicist Schumann in 1952. He mathematically predicted that the most predominant standing wave resonates around 7.8 Hz. The amazing fact is that this frequency is identical to the Alpha spectrum of human brain waves.

Alfa Brainwaves and Meditative States

When a person is meditating, praying or deeply relaxed his brain resonates within Alpha and Theta rhythms range of 4-8 Hz. During this relaxed state of mind, waves of Alpha and Theta frequencies cascade across our entire brain, making it possible for the human being and our dear planet Earth to come into resonance. Was this the vibration that ancient sages of India called AUM (Om), the sacred sound of creation? Or perhaps the original Sound of God that was mentioned in Bible? The scientists believe that these waves help regulate our bodies' internal clock, improve sleep patterns, and hormonal secretion.

Schumann Resonance and Healers

For a decade, Dr Robert Beck from US researched the brain wave activity of healers from various backgrounds. He examined Christian healers, shamans, dowsers, wicca practitioners, etc. and each exhibited 'nearly identical EEG signatures' during healing of a 7.8-8Hz brainwave activity. It appears that the basic earth's frequency of 7.8Hz can enhance growth, improve immune responses, and generally rebalance the human body.

Schumann Resonance and Spiritual Practices

Various spiritual practices and spiritual paths and rituals are designed to allow this magic meditative Alpha range to rain. Bells ringing, shamanic drumming, mantra chanting, trance dance, meditation, various salutations to God, healing dances, Christian singing, bolster the human brain's ancient harmonization with the planetary field. Entrainment happens when vibrations of one object cause the vibrations of another object to oscillate at the same rate. Our brain waves are prone to this synchronisation, and external rhythms have a direct effect on our mood, thoughts, emotions and re-action.

Alpha to Delta Brainwaves

Alpha waves (7-13 cycles per second) are present during dreaming, deep relaxation, and meditation. Scientists claim that in Alpha, we are more open to the wealth of creativity, we feel happier, regenerated, and in tune. C.M. Anderson, M.D. (1998) of Harvard links a persistent internally generated sound of 'humming insects' that many people experience within Churches or Temples, during meditation or during deep intense experiences, to the Alpha 10Hz rhythm. Indian Yogis, gurus and sages associate this sound to deep meditation and Samadhi experiences.

Just to give you an idea of other frequencies, Delta waves are the slowest but highest in amplitude (between 0-4 Hz) and Theta waves (4-7 cycles per second) are abundant in deep dreamless sleep and in the deep meditation. Theta has also been identified as the gateway to learning and memory, it is the slow activity often connected with creativity, intuition, trance, and unconsciousness. It is the state of mind where we focus inwardly experiencing contemplation and silence.

Beta is a 'fast' activity, present when we are alert while Gamma relates to integrated thoughts, information rich task processing.

Schumann Resonance, Yin and Yang of Creation

Mankind developed with two subtle environmental signals, the Chinese call them Yin and Yang.

The Yang Alpha frequency of the Schumann wave, and the Beta Yin frequency of our waking consciousness.

Our brain dances amongst these important rhythms changing its functions every 1 to 2 hours, Yogis and Scientists see these happenings observing the dominant nostril exchange, the exchange of the Ida and Pingala energy flow, or left versus right brain dominance. Alpha waves are induced by calmness, inner awareness, creativity and learning while Beta is where our normal waking consciousness is, where we have active thoughts processes switched on, with outer awareness, automatic responses and emotions. It ranges from 13-30Hz.

16Hz is a bottom limit of our normal hearing. Piano's notes have frequencies from 27.5 to 4,186Hz. Female speech is within the frequency of 140 to 500Hz, Male speech hits the frequency of 80 to 240Hz.

30 to 60Hz is within Gamma Range and it is switched on during the danger, it is our brain's decision making process when we are within 'flight or fight' responses.

Ranges from 33-50Hz are associated with many spiritual phenomena: awakening of chakras, sensitive consciousness, it is supposed to be the Pyramid frequency (inside). This frequency is also associated with our learning and thinking processes that require full concentration and alertness. It occurs when the body is relaxed but the mind is in a state of high focus.

Today, modern medicine uses various frequencies for healing, and within our ancient past temples were build with the acoustical resonances around 90 - 111Hz in mind. This is the frequency that induces the production of beta endorphins within our brain responsible for the feeling of happiness well-being and balance. 126Hz is associated with Sun, 420Hz with the Moon.

Very low musical sounds can have very long wavelengths: some central Javanese (from Indonesia) gongs vibrate at around 8 Hz to 10 Hz.

Healing with Sound and 528 Hz. 528Hz also called The Love Frequency

A regular piano 'C' or 'Do' vibrates to a frequency of 512Hz, and the 'C' of 528Hz has been a part of an ancient scale called the Solfeggio Scale. 528Hz is known as the 'miracle' tone. The difference in the frequencies is due to different tuning methods utilized in ancient times.

According to Dr. Leonard Horowitz, 528Hz is a frequency that is central to the 'musical mathematical matrix of creation'. He explained that NASA studies show that the sun's output contains 528Hz as 'a central frequency within it.' He claims that this frequency can be found in oxygen as a result of the photosynthesis of plants. A math scientist Victor Showell describes 528Hz as essential to the ancient Phi, and the Golden Mean. Dr Emoto in his 'Water Research' showed that water molecules that are exposed to the frequency of 528Hz create beautiful crystal shapes.

Dr. Horowitz observed that the frequency can be found in sounds such as laughter, sighing, and yawning. According to him we emit this frequency when we experience unconditional love, and compassion.

Goddess Worship Rituals within Malta Temples

Walking back 7,000 years...

The temples were built from stones as huge as 19 tones! Today we find more than 30 megalithic on a small island of Malta in the middle of Mediterranean. Who were they, the civilization that left these architecture miracles? Were these temples of giants? Or was this little island a pilgrimage site? Did we have people coming from far to worship the Goddess?

Sleeping Lady from Hypogeum Malta Underground Temple

Statues found dating back 5,000 years ago suggest a concept of asexual God or Goddess, worshiping Divine that goes beyond sexuality.

The structures, we know today are aligned to the Sun. During the equinoxes, the sun rays walk through the Temple's portal blessing the altars. We find deliberate polarity within the Temples, the Female and Male aspect of creation is equally worshiped.

Water and Earth was worshiped on 1 side of the Temples and Air and Fire on the other side, grouping the elements into female and male manifestations of creation. All the ancient philosophies resonate with this sacred wisdom: Yin and Yang of Taoists, Ida and Pingala of Yogis, merge of Black King and White Queen of Alchemists, Kabbhala's Tree of Life and its female and male path to understanding the creation.

The temples welcome us with the full light of the sun, leading us to the reflected light symbolising the light of the moon, and presenting us with the complete darkness that takes us into our souls' meditations.

Evidence suggests that the temples were also aligned to the Moon and the Stars.

Hypogeum Malta Underground temple dates back to 4-5,000BC

Listening to messages that Temples provide we link to the spiritual messages from the religions from all around the world.

Descending into the underground temples, we descend through the spiral into the Earth, into the Earth's womb. Descending into the centre of Earth we go deep down, 11 meters into the Earth.

We find the Oracle Room and the room called Holy of Holies. The Oracle Room resembles the womb, it is round and full of red spirals and the Holy of Holies is strongly geometrically shaped, with very precise lines and square altars.

Temples and Initiations

Knocking at the door of eternity, looking at the oldest free standing structures, temples, on Earth we observe symbols and discover secrets so that we apply them within our spiritual practices.

Temples are shaped like Goddess, with trees, animals and spirals carved on the stones. Mystical spiral is everywhere within the temples. Spiral as the symbol of our path to consciousness, from unit point of consciousness, from God within that is expanding to eternity to the transcendent omnipresent, omnipotent God or Goddess.

Descending into the underground, priests and priestesses use chanting to reach alter state of consciousness, to become Divine, reconnect Heaven and Earth.

This place is a magical place of dreams, visions and mystical chants, where Priests and Priestesses go into the Oracle, into dream states of consciousness, using musical rituals to reach higher states of consciousness.

Ancient Temples Symbols, Worship Sound Rituals

John tells us: 'In the beginning was the Word, and the Word was with God, and the Word was God'. Upanishads (a sacred Hindu text) say that the divine, all-encompassing consciousness first manifested as sound 'OM', the vibration of the Supreme. Everything has its own frequency. Pythagoras created his musical scale starting with a note A (just next to the middle C) that resonates at the frequency of 111Hz. Perhaps this one note contains many overtones like white light that contains all the colours. Perhaps it is a Cosmic 'I love you' that is within all of us. 111Hz is a frequency of a low male voice.

Paul Devereux is a professor from Cambridge and an archaeo-acoustician who researches the area of archaeology and acoustics and who has visited ancient sites and temples analysing the ritual use of sound. He's discovered that burial mounds in Ireland called Cairns, even though they are made of different materials, and are different sizes, all resonate at one particular frequency, of: 111 Hz. He has decided to take it a step further and explore what happens to the brain when it is exposed to the frequency of 111Hz. Findings of MRI scans suggest that at exactly 111hz, the brain switches off the prefrontal cortex, deactivating the language centre, and temporary switches from left to right-sided dominance, that is responsible for intuition, creativity, holistic processing, inducing a state of meditation or a trance.

Further research directed by Prof. Robert Jahn has tested acoustic behaviour in megalithic sites in the UK, showing that they sustained a strong resonance at a sound frequency between 95 and 120 hertz.

Divine Healing Frequency and Malta Temples

The Maltese Hypogeum is a temple hewn out of the rock during 3600-2500BC that covers some 500m2 with the lowest room being around 11 metres under the ground, mirroring Temples above the ground that are the oldest free standing structures on Earth. Testing that analysed the sound within the Oracle Chamber in the Hypogeum found to match the same pattern of resonance at the frequency of 111Hz.

Hypogeum Malta Underground Temple Holy of Holiest

Seven thousand years ago, a thousand years before the Egyptian pyramids, in the Mediterranean, in Malta, an amazing culture seemed to be flourishing in peace and harmony for 2,500 years. Within the remains of their times, no evidence of weapons, or defensive architecture was found. The bones analysis suggests a healthy population. Their cult seems to have rituals that are life affirming, earth and nature oriented, worshipping Great God/dess, experiencing the divine as both feminine and male, attuning to the natural rhythms and cycles of Sun, Moon and Earth, and the change of the seasons. These Neolithic people were certainly not savage cavemen.

Healing with Sound and Inducing Higher State of Consciousness

So, 7,000 years ago, a culture that settled in Malta, and built Maltese Megalithic Temples, had an advance knowledge not only of architecture but of sound rituals that induce a trance-like meditation or higher state of consciousness. It is likely that the sound ritual was used to lead 'devotees' into trance-like meditation, increasing their emotional and social intelligence. Today, various studies suggest that the long-term practice of meditation may sculpt the brain towards more patient, emotionally balanced, and creative individuals.

Descending into Hypogeum one can re-connect with this culture that used overtone chanting, unearthly, angelic singing, bell ringing, singing balls, drums to reach altered states of consciousness. These sacred musical rituals found their place in religions all around the world: within Christian Mass singing, Tibetan or Buddhist chanting, Hindu devotional songs. The sound resonates through the bones within Hypogeum and people from all over the known world may have used the island as a centre of their mystical practices, a pilgrims' site, coming to worship their beloved Goddess, coming to experience Divine.

Serpent Priests of Maya, Egypt and Malta

Within the Hypogeum, a number of lengthened skulls, called the dolichocephalous skulls were found. The skulls were found near a sacred well dedicated to the Mother Goddess together with the small statue of a sleeping goddess with a snake engraving on it.

The symbolism of snake is wisdom, health, and esoteric knowledge.

It is interesting that in Lower Egypt, the pharaoh's symbol is a bee. Malta's ancient name is 'Melita', the Latin word for honey. The 'serpent priest' tradition is also found in the Middle East, Kurdistan, where at around 5,000BC we find the goddesses represented with faces of vipers and lengthened heads.

In Egypt, Pharaoh Akhenaton (around 1350 BC) and his royal family, were portrayed as people with lengthened head and snake-like faces. The X-rays of Tuthankamon's skull, Akhenaton's son, showed a dolichocephalous cranium.

When Saint Paul shipwrecked in Malta, he writes that a snake bit his foot... This could have been one of the last 'serpent priests' of the Goddess on the island.

Gnostic Cosmology, by Nuit from Art of 4 Elements (AoL #2)

At its birth
descending into the sea of time and space
a Soul goes through the ladder of seven spheres
Reaching Earth it is coarsened by planets' touch

On its pilgrimage back - it rises
using the same ladder
merging with the planets - one by one

It takes a sweat bath with Saturn
through a vale of tears that extracts
what is best within spirit, mind and life

Then Jupiter takes its turn
promising good fortune, health and wealth
multiplying - he binds it to Maya's fighting birds
tamas, rajas and satwa are their names

Mars brings fire - and sword and shield
his fury heightened, his goal is clear
more transparent & subtle realm

The Sun rides a lion
appearing mighty, strong and free
cleansing the soul from arrogance, vanity and pride

Venus gives pleasure & unimaginable joy
Coming on a peacock tail - sensual, and royal
checking immodesty traces and maya comprehension ploy

In Mercury's embrace the Soul falls, now pure and virginal
the matter solidified - fire indestructible
Phoenix rises from its funeral flames

Luna receives an immaculate, purple robed King
giving It the final sublimation
Pelican, with her blood, feeds her dead young back to life

From Alfa to Omega, from metal to Gold, from Soul to Spirit
Until the Serpent has swallowed

its-own tail

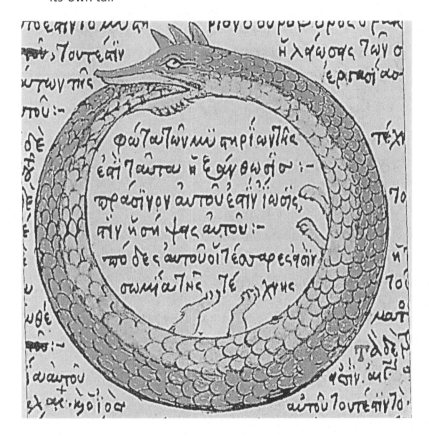

Ouroboros image 1478 drawing by Theodoros Pelecanos, of an alchemical tract attributed to Synesius

Middle Bronze Age Goddess 1800 BC

Ever since its first discovery in 1908 by the Serbian archaeologist Miloje Vasić, Vinča culture, a Neolithic settlement that spanned most of Serbia, parts of Romania, Bulgaria & Macedonia, has been of great interest to the lay public and scientists alike.

From Neolithic monuments to Roman Villas and prehistoric figurines the river basin of Danube (Serbia, Romania, Bulgaria) has proved rich for treasure hunters over the years

Vinča European Civilization

Research and analysis of the artifacts, remains of houses, show a civilization that was so advance to have insulation against the elements, multi-room layouts, even public communal spaces. Divided by streets, enclosed by ditches discovered all over Serbia in numerous archaeological sites.

The sheer number of objects found at the Vinča sites, suggest an ancient export or ancient industrial production. In its times of plenty the Vinča culture's scientists have developed metallurgy. "There is a wider flow of people and ideas in a larger geographic area. Obsidian from the Carpathian mountains, shells from the Aegean and Black seas, axes from the rare Alpine rock nephrite, and the salt trade is also confirmed," Dr Petrović says about the flow of people and goods. This period of Vinča history shows trading connections with other parts of Europe as metal objects began to be exported from Vinča.

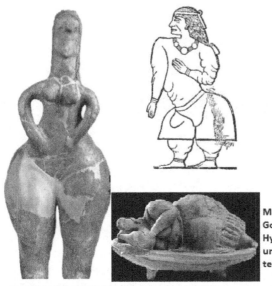

Maltese Temples Goddess found in Hypogeum, underground temple 3,500 BC

Neolithic Europe The Female Figurine, 6,500 BC
Serbia

Female Goddess found on the Neolithic Europe site dated 6,000 BC in Donja Branjevina, Maltese Goddess 3,000BC & Eli Egyptian Fat Queen brought from Journey to the Land of Punt (Egyptian Tomb Painting) 2,700BC

Župa Goddess 6000 years old Vinča Serbia

Last year, archaeologists led by Sanja Crnobrnja Krasić found a most amazing 6,000-year-old monumental figurine representing a fertility goddess named „Venus of Župa". „This discovery proves our assumption that Vitkovo was a religious centre of the Vinča culture, because the Venus figurine is tall more than 30 centimeters."

Marija Gimbutas (1921 – 1994) was a Lithuanian archeologist known for her research into the Neolithic and Bronze Age cultures of Old Eurlope. During the 1950s and early 1960s, Gimbutas earned a reputation as a world-class specialist on Bronze Age Europe, she directed major excavations of Neolithic sites in southeastern Europe including Anzabegovo, near Štip, Republic of Macedonia, and Sitagroi in Thessaly (Greece). In her work she reinterpreted European prehistory and challenged many traditional assumptions about the beginnings of European civilization.

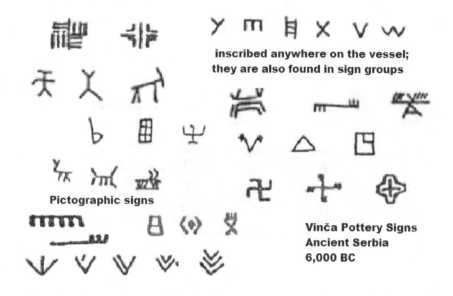

inscribed anywhere on the vessel; they are also found in sign groups

Pictographic signs

Vinča Pottery Signs
Ancient Serbia
6,000 BC

Vincha symbols Ancient Serbia 6,000 BC

As a Professor of European Archaeology and Indo-European Studies she unearthed a great number of artifacts which she researched and documented throughout her career.

„Fertility is not a primary function of the prehistoric Goddess Creatrix and has nothing to do with sexuality."

„The prehistoric Goddess of the Upper Palaeolithic and Neolithic essentially is a tri-functional goddess: Life-giver, Death, Death-wielder and Regenerator."

„To the first function belong such images as the anthropomorphic and zoomorphic (deer, bear) Giver of Birth, Cosmic Creatrix and Giver-of-All in the form of water fowl and water fowl-woman hybrids and serpent woman, as well as protectresses of young life (Nurse and Madonna)"

„death and regeneration (the two are closely linked), belong the Vulture - Owl- and other Bird of Prey-Goddesses, anthropomorphic Stiff Nude, bone phalange, triangle and hourglass shapes (sometimes portrayed with bird's claws instead of human feet or hands"

"the Goddess as Regenerative Uterus in zoomorphic shapes (bucranium, fish, frog, hedgehog), and Rising Goddess as an insect (bee, butterfly) and a life column (tree, snake)"

„The moon's three phases - new, waxing, and old - are repeated in trinities or triple-functional deities that recall moon phases : maiden, nymph, and crone; life-giving, death-giving, and transformational; rising, dying, and self-renewing. Life-givers are also death-wielders. Immortality is secured through the innate forces of regeneration within Nature itself."

„The Pregnant Goddess is one of the stereotypes among the upper palaeolithic divine images repeatedly produced through time."

"Good examples of this stereotype are known from Kostienki I in the Ukraine and from La Marche, Vienne, France. Kostienki sculptures may date from around 20,000 B.C."

"Their breasts and buttocks are the focus of attention, not their bellies; they hold their hands on their breasts. The images we shall be concerned with here are of pregnant women holding their hands on their bellies."

"In the Copper Age, the Pregnant Goddess remains one of the most revered divine characters : She is the only one portrayed enthroned in a regal posture; her bulging belly and other generous body parts are marked by squares, triangles, snake coil spirals, and the numbers two and four."

"The lozenge and triangle with one or more dots are encountered on shrine walls, vases, seals, and typically on the pregnant belly or other parts of the Pregnant Goddess, starting in the 7th millennium B.C"

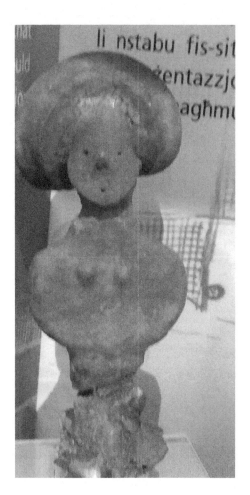

A Maltese statue of Goddess, Archaeology Museum, Valletta

"If the head is shown, it is cylindrical and wears a mask, which is not beaked but human, with a normal mouth. Removable masks as found at Achilleion II and IV (c. 6300-5900 B.C.) probably belong to the same Goddess."

Placing Goddess Figurines within Houses

"In Old European settlements, figurines of this type are located on a platform near the oven or other area of grain preparation, and under the floor, whereas the Bird Goddess is characteristically found inside house shrines. The earliest evidence for this distribution comes from the

Achilleion mound, c. 6500-5600 B.C., Thessaly, northern Greece (author's excavation; Gimbutas 1988)."

"In several instances, enthroned figurines of the 5th millennium B.C. are found in hidden alcoves or pits beneath dwelling floors "

European Cross – or sowing in four directions

"The lozenge with a dot in the four corners may denote planting "in all four directions", a concept still extant in European folk belief. Throughout Europe, sowing in four directions is a ceremony carried out at the winter and spring plantings to ensure that dead vegetation will come to life again."

"Greece, pots with corn seeds kept near the hearth in the house symbolized the dead who rest in the womb (pot) and are resurrected in the spring. The dead were called "Demetrioi", those who belong to Demeter, the Grain Mother, and who rest, like the corn, in the womb of that goddess."

"Traditionally, three and nine (three times three) were magical numbers used to invoke increase and multiplication."

"The bread oven was the principal feature of Old European temples. Some miniature shrine models, such as the one from Popudnia in the western Ukraine, contain one or more figurines engaged in the baking activities of grinding grain and preparing dough. The inner walls of the model are painted with a multiple lozenge design, clearly linking the shrine with figurines so marked. Bread prepared in a temple was sacred bread, dedicated to a Goddess and used in her rituals.

Sacred Bread from Banjica 3500 BC

In later antiquity, bread and cakes for religious purposes were baked in various shapes - loaf, snake, bird, animal, flower - or had an impressed design. There is no doubt that this custom is Neolithic in origin, and it is highly probable that Neolithic seals with various raised or incised symbols were to stamp the appropriate design on the breads and cakes assigned to a particular Goddess."

Sacred hills

"This symbol - a hill - shaped figure with a small knob at the top – is repeated in an engraving on a slab at the beginning of the passage."

"Sacred hills were venerated in history up to the 20th century. The worship of the Earth Mother was celebrated on mountain summits crowned with large stones. Such practices are recorded for both Minoan and modern Crete in the south, the British Isles in the west, and the East Baltic area in the east, in various historical periods. In Germany and the Scandinavian countries, flat stones with polished surfaces are widely known as Brautsteine, or bridestones."

Large Stones as Goddesses

"Large stones with flat surfaces dedicated to Ops Consiua, a Roman Goddess of Earth Fertility, were kept in holes in the ground (sub terra) covered with straw. They were uncovered only once a year during a harvest feast (Dumézil 1969: 293-296). About 1500 years later, the same tradition is recorded in northern Europe. In Lithuania, the Jesuit annals of 1600 A.D. describe large stones with flat surfaces dug into the earth and covered with straw; they were called Deyves, "Goddesses" (Annuae Litterae) Societatis Jesii , anni 1600 ; cited by Greimas 1979 : 215). Thus we learn that the stone is the Goddess herself."

Primordial Womb and Red

"The caves, crevices, and caverns of the earth are natural manifestations of the primordial womb of the Mother. This idea is not Neolithic in origin; it goes back to the Palaeolithic, when the narrow passages, oval-shaped areas, clefts, and small cavities of caves are marked or painted entirely in red (Leroi-Gourhan 1967 :174). This red color must have symbolized the color of the Mother's regenerative organs. In southern and southeastern Europe, neolithic graves were oval in shape, symbolic of an egg or womb."

Vinča statue twins 3200 BC

Number Two and Goddess, Vinca twins is a female figurine from the culture of Old Europe Vinča.

Archaeological finds in Vinča include incredible stone statues used for Neolithic rituals and burials go back to 4,000 BC. The Twins, belonging to the Vinca settlement, was unearthed in what is now the area's Heritage Park and dates back 5,200 years.

Since Ancient Europeans followed the river Danube of north Serbia numerous generations of humans have made the county their home and left behind intriguing artefacts for 21st century archeologists to discover. The statues dug up by the Serbian and International researchers would not have been touched by humans for thousands of years and offer a fascinating insight into ancient Europe's rituals, and development of thought.

Number Two as the repetition that brings plenty or a philosophical concept later developed by Pythagoras and Neo-Platonists Numbers...

"The rock-cut tombs and hypogea of Malta, Sicily, and Sardinia are usually uterine, egg-shaped, or roughly anthropomorphic. In Western Europe, where large stones were used in grave architecture, the body of the Goddess is magnificently "cruciform" and realized "double-oval" as the megalithic tombs tomb. are unmistakably The so-called human-shaped. The stone temples of Malta share the same contours as terracotta and stone figurines of the Goddess."

"The twin or seasonal (mother-daughter, summer-winter) aspect of the Goddess very probably is also expressed by the double temples of Malta such at Ggantija and Mnajdra"

Neolithic women from Pontokomi Eordaias, Greece, in the Archaeological Museum of Aiani

"Four other vases are decorated with the egg and seed symbol flanked by snake spirals. The design on the eight vases is remarkable for its thematic unity and the use of the traditional "power of two" device - repetition - in the conventional way to express (and to invoke) fertility."

Sacred holes in Temples

"partition walls sometimes have round holes. Such holes are also present in Maltese temples. Their meaning is apparent if the still-extant veneration of stones with holes is considered. Belief in the miraculous power of holed stones occurs in Ireland, Scotland, England, France, and in many other European countries. Crawling through an aperture of a sacred stone brought regeneration; diseases and sins were discarded."

"Buttocks were also portrayed in that most precious material, gold. Gold-plated amulets in the shape of buttocks and buttocks in repoussée or punctated line on gold plate are known from Copper Age Hungary and Romania. Similar intensification can be seen in energy symbols - whirls and double snake spirals - on the egg-shaped buttocks of figurines from the Karanovo, Cucuteni, and Vinca groups."

Writing in Neolithic Europe Vinča Serbia Danube 5,300 BC

Fragment of a clay vessel with an M-shaped incision Neolithic Europe Vinča Serbia Danube 5,300 BC

Wisdom of Symbols of the oldest Neolithic Culture in Vinča, Europe

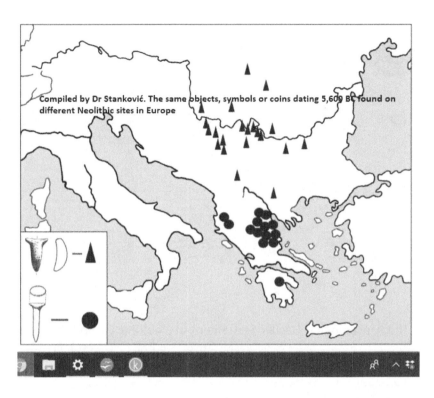

Neolithic Europe coins or ritual objects Ancient Europe 5,500 BC map compiled by Dr Stankovic

"DatDas organizes a catalogue of 5,421 actual signs. These are recorded from a corpus of 1,178 inscriptions composed of two or more signs and 971 inscribed artifacts (some finds have two or more inscriptions)."

21 Stamps dating 5,600 BC discovered in Vinča, Archeological Findings of Neolithic Europe

"Stamps carrying spirals, zigzags, crosses, and dots decorated storage vessels, hearth rims, frying pans and exported pottery." Younger, 1992.

The Archeological Hacilar Settlement of Neolithic Europe dated to 6,000 BC and the Stamps

Nea Nikomedia clay seals assemblage consists of almost all the shapes and 10 of 21 ornaments that have circulated in the Balkans in the Early Neolithic period. The archeologists cannot as yet decipher the messages passed with these stamps connecting the settlements within a hundreds or even more than a thousand kilometers. The symbols were associated with prestigious locations or items within the sites.

The motifs on Early Neolithic stamps in the Balkans were more heterogeneous. It can be indicative that the Balkan patterns regularly consist of zigzags, spirals, dots and labyrinth patterns.

Some of the "comb" or "brush" symbols, most likely have represented numbers and both Serbian and worldwide archeologists agree that the fact that more than a quarter of the inscriptions are located on the bottom of pots indicate that symbols were primarily numbers, the goods description or the names of the owners of the pots (those days Kings or Rulers), or Gods (Priests). With the Neolithic Europe, within the Mediterranean advanced civilizations, the use of symbols by the

Minoans and Sumerians was also used for trade. The Vinča culture appears to have traded its goods widely with other cultures.

Old European Script of Kurgan Culture 5,400 BC

Marija Gimbutas has named the neolithic script "Old European Script", and has championed the term "Kurgan culture" an archaeological expression of the Proto-Indo-Europeans. This amazing Old European civilization, has occupied the area from Danube (now Serbia, Bulgaria, Romania, Greece, Macedonia) down to the Mediterranean Sicily Crete line. Gimbutas observed that neolithic European iconography was predominantly female, she called it "matristic" (woman-centred, not necessarily matriarchal) culture that worshipped various gods and goddesses. The scientific research of Winn Shan tells us that Vinča logographics have now been found on an area of Serbia, southeaster Hungary, western Romania, and western Bulgaria.

Tartaria tablets unearthed near Tartaria, Romania

Acknowledging my nationality as Serbian and Maltese, this research gives me further excitement, for linking Maltese Neolithic's with Serbian ones, bring us – Arabs, Ethiopian, Chinese, European, African, one step closer to each other. A deliberate dis-empowerment or destruction of arts, books, historical facts, is painful and when it is done to protect trade or billionaires' businesses, the female within me, the one that has started this move towards knowledge and civilizations 5,000 BC, that passed the commandment – "Do Not Kill", that had preferred trade and rituals instead of wars, that moved all of us towards knowledge / writing / script, through the spiral journey of consciousness development wishes to be recognized.

Until recently I did not know that Constantine the Great (of Constantinople) was from Niš (Serbia), that Aleksandar the Great's mother Hellena was from Serbia, that the territory of now Serbia was the center of the Orphic tradition led by Pythagoras, that Macedonians (as Ancient Greeks or Ancient Slavs or Ancient Arabs) were an active and advanced actor, living in the cross-road of the Neolithic European Civilization of the Danube with the Egyptian Kingdom.

Today we enter the mind-chita of the scientists and consciousness researchers or respectable human beings no-matter where we are from, no-matter of our DNA patterns, and within this vibration we stay in owe of Babylon, Ancient Greece, Maltese Temples, Ancient China, Cyprus Civilization, or Serbian Vinča.

Barberians of South East Europe

Scythian Warriors Kurgan burial near Kerch Hermitage Museum Saint Petersburg 450 BC

It was Barbarians that worship Bog (a Slavic name for God) and have said Jai to Vo (Bull) within the word DjaVo (devil). It was Barberians that have passed the knowledge of Amorites, Babylon, Pythagoras within the same region.

Natural Migration that has happened in Europe

The migration has shifted the borders of each country or nation, in Europe, up towards the north, yet none can truly say when the migration has really happened. In the 13th century Slavs on the Balkan were so established that they had their own monasteries, schools, Kings, Town-Kingdoms, yet at most of the places they were slaves to the Austro-Hungarian or the Ottoman Empire. My father who is from Montenegro and Mostar (Herzegovina), a most wonderful little town in Bosnia, had an exact profile one will find within a typical ancient Greek sculpture, which of course proves nothing, but it does make one wonder... We, in Serbia, get so deeply hurt if any of the Ancient Greek monuments is damaged, we speak of Greece as of our home-land, loving everything that is Greek. Greece doesn't quite know that we even exist, more that an annoying neighbor that in case of Macedonia wish to claim the Ancient Macedonian name, sharing deep subconscious love with ancient Logos, Philosophy, Athena, etc.

As nomads, most of us have already had a migration journey from one country to another, this knowledge is already within our bloods, or we have married an African Shaman, or like in my case, have adopted kids from Ethiopia, so our souls dance with the rain-bow colors of many different cultural influences. Vibrating the Cosmic spiral rhythm of the Universe, I can only feel deeply sorry for the Humanity's misconceptions about Race Superiority or Chosen Race that has exploited the South of our planet for far too long.

There are 21 discovered symbols / stamps within Ancient Vinča culture Distributed as a Spiral within its Settlements

Can this be a coincidence? Some millennia later our priests have told us about the 21 + 1 that is silent, that represents God as no-sound, that has trinity of sounds within its make-up (Y+H+W), that could be a vowel. Our ancients have started with 22 Arabic consonants, there are 22 sacred Hebrew letters, through the trade, the Ancient Chinese have passed the numbers 1-10 as sacred symbols, within their philosophical set-up of Taoism as Yin and Yang, a male and female representation of Cosmos, that within forces manifest as 10 symbols x 2 = 20 + 1 that is Tao (Yin and Yang combined) the same as the one found in Egyptian / Phoenician alphabet, or Jewish Kabbalah, that within its wisdom talk about God, creation, divine, Tao, Female and Male consciousness manifestation forces, Kundalini awakening with its journey back to God.

This development of sounds as frequencies within our own languages has already happened some 2,000s of years before Christ. Within my work of mapping Serbian (viewing it as ancient Slavic) to Chinese (no doubt that it kept its ancient wisdom within its symbols) to Arabic (classical Arabic that is spoken in Malta) to Ancient Greek (for Latin goes back only 2 millenniums) to Hebrew, we are knocking at the door of Ancient Sacred Languages and Sounds of Gods.

Viewing the languages of all of us, as a Sacred Instrument of God, exploring the mystical knowledge of frequencies, we will totally understand why of the Western languages, English and Spanish are the most spoken on our little planet, one leading to RiCH, HaVe, GooGle, YaHoo, Coco CHaNeL, GuCi, MuSiC StaRS explosions, while understanding the Human Mind that still very much globally subconsciously worship the names of Gods.

Runes are an alphabetic script, called fuþark, used among Germanic tribes

What scientists are after are abecedaries (passed through Europe as a script). Longer time period, more difficult the find. I.e. many inscriptions exist in younger fuþark, and there are only about 430 in older fuþark, used until 700 AC, of which only 17 contain complete, or incomplete abecedaries. Less than 100 span from 300 AC to 700 AC creating what is known as the South-Germanic corpus.

A researcher can easily imagine that the most scripts found would belong to our wealthy and influential men's graves (in Balkan read: Germanic or Ottoman or Byzantine).

During the last 2,000 years, the only women buried were Queens or Saints, surely not slaves. In Balkans, since Slavs were slaves, changing the names to reflect the power-God-Goddess structure (for example Dio-nisus. or Herodotus, or St Whoever Christian Name) was common.

What has survived came from the scripts found on metal objects in 600 AC graves containing personal names. It is a typical example of an Early Slavic settlement of the 6-700 AC. The same ones you find following the river Danube. The above mentioned rib bone fragment, originates from Břeclav Lány in South Moravia, Czechia

Codex Runicus, a vellum manuscript from c. 1300 containing one of the oldest and best preserved texts of the Scanian law (Skånske lov), written entirely in runes.

The first written reports about Slavs, referred to Slavs as Sclavini, and their attacks on the Byzantine & later Ottoman Empire during the 600 AC – 1,500 AC. Early written mentions of Slavs include Sclauos in the 777AC, 805 AC, 822 AC, 855AC, etc.

This rune-inscribed fragment of a bone could be the first archaeological evidence for a direct contact between Germanic and Early Slavic tribes in Europe from the late 600 BC found in any Slavic settlement said the groundbreaking report.

As often happens with important archaeological discoveries, the Lany bone may shed light on old historical mysteries but also raises new questions that could open up enticing avenues of research.

One interesting puzzle facing scholars is to figure out why a Germanic script ended up being used in a Slavic setting. There is a possibility that it was written by Slavs who learned it from a Germanic tribe, or the Germanic people have learned it from the Slavs.

It is a tantalizing question that might not be solved for unfortunately, the Lany bone is the only physical evidence to date of writing among early Slavs.

This ancient system consisted of 24 letters.

The Serbian Vinča's (A Danube settlement spanning 6,000 years in Neolithic Europe's Serbia) sculptures, artifacts have used symbols for religious purposes, and these were always placed in a particular manner around the head of the sculpture.

The Egyptian script had used symbols for magical purposes.

Slavs with their maternal culture mainly used cremation graves, a few burned bones and pots. The inscription would have been on wood and burnt. Machacek suggests that the discovery of the Lany bone could eventually resonate far beyond the halls of academia.

According to some anthropologists, there is no evidence for a mass migration of Slavs through Europe. According to many linguists, by 1,000 AC, Slavic speakers were all around Europe, switching languages from Greek or German or Roman to Slavic.

"In the central Danube region, for instance, Germanic, Avar and Slavic settlement followed each other very closely in time... As defined by M. Parczewski (2004) based on finds from Ukraine and Poland, typical Early Slavic settlements

i) are located on the edge of a river valleys,

ii) allowed for a self-sufficient lifestyle, and

iii) consisted of small sunken-floor huts with a stone or clay oven and built on a square plan.

iv) cremation was the predominant funeral rite, and

v) no well-developed handicrafts other than rudimentary iron works and handmade undecorated pottery of the Prague type existed."

Gaia has unfortunately passed through a destruction of gigantic proportions, the 1st and 2nd World War, shaking the Europe's, Balkan's or Polish Lands where this particular ancient Slavic ruin had been discovered. Now, imagine this, how much we must honor our young or old archeology graduates, working in the field, researchers who fully comprehend how meticulously rare markings of any sorts are.

An Ancient Debate

It had long been believed that the Orthodox Serbian (Macedonian) Christian missionaries Cyril and Methodius have introduced a writing system, now called Cyrillic, now used only in Greece, Serbia, Macedonia, and Russia during the 900 AC. Slavs that have been converted to Roman Catholic fate and Islam have started using Glagolitic script instead. But this date is some 300 years after the inscription on the Lany bone, which has been dated using genetic and radiocarbon methods to around 600 AC.

The idea that Slavs had learned writing earlier has long been a matter of debate.

As far back as the 19th century, Slavonic scholars had explored the idea that Slavs had already achieved literacy in the pre-Christian era.

One of the main cornerstones of the argument is a text from 900 AC by a Slavic Bulgarian scholar/monk named Chernorizets Hrabar. Hrabar in Serbian literally means "Courageous" for he indeed needed courage to portray this line of thought.

He made reference to a system of writing using "strokes and incisions" adopted by the early Slavs.

However, there is a twist to this interesting scientific tale.

How an "alien alphabet" in 600 AC came to be adopted (used by Priests or Kings for only kings or priests had any form of education) by these early Slavs if the so-called "great migration" of Slavic peoples had just happened.

The runic script has historically only been associated with Germanic tribes.

Ancient China & Symbols

Any discussion of early writing brings up the question of what IS writing? The Western civilizations' researcher will all agree that writing is a way of presenting language using alphabetic, i.e. phonetic symbols. Based on sound, rather that an image, individual letters or syllables represent this sound. The Eastern civilizations' researcher, that had various ways of writing since 5,000 BC would see symbols as writings.

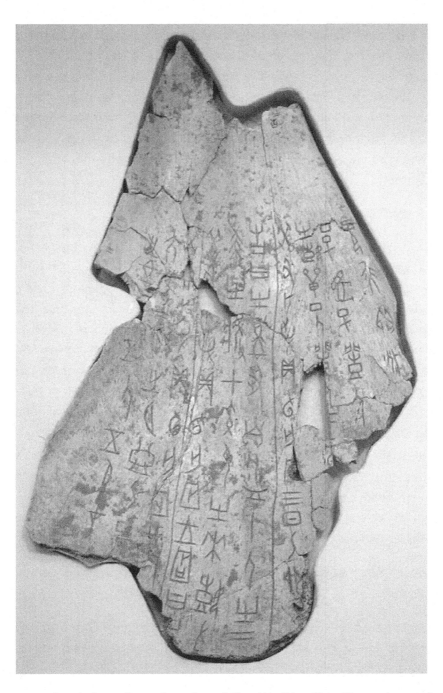

Oracle bone from the reign of King Wu Ding (late Shang dynasty), 5,000 BC

Finding "the language of the gods" based on Root Sounds or Vibrations of the Universe, in a mission of discovering this speech of the Universe, could help a man understand a meaning of a language without ever studying it. Wouldn't that be just amazing! A man's mind is both consciously and subconsciously capable of hearing these sounds and matching them with a symbol. For example the Arabic "Ra", connects us with the sound of Sun, as much as "Ma" connects us with the symbol of a Mother.

Ancient Chinese Alphabet Symbols

While exploring the Chinese characters I was mesmerized by the beauty and wisdom hidden within the ancient characters. Now imagine this, to be able to read a child in school needs to learn over 3,000 characters and if ones wishes to study philosophy in Chinese, we step into the world of 35,000 unique characters. What has fascinated me most, is that each drawn character builds a unique story, beauty will speak of a beauty of a flower, or an artwork or youth. What most of us do not know is that apart from the amazing world of pictures that is equally readable to a Chinese or a Japanese or a Korean scholar, we also get a sort of phonetic compounds. Examples are 河he "river", 湖hu "lake", 滑hua "slippery". All these characters have on the left a radical of three short strokes (氵), which is a reduced form of shuei that is water. So, if we travel back to the ancient alphabet, the one that was used to write prayers, ritual, or messages to after-world Gods, we come to some inspiring findings.

Cangjie 2,500 BC is Chinese characters Science Recognized Official Inventor

Cangjie (2650 BC) lived in ancient China at the time of the Yellow Emperor and was his official historian. Such an advanced civilization, to have an Official Historian!

Ancient Chinese B (Sun shines over an object, Rising Sun) for Bright, Beautiful, Bella, Beo, aBjaD (white in Arabic), Buono, Bog (God in Slavic), Bene-Volent (of many cultures)

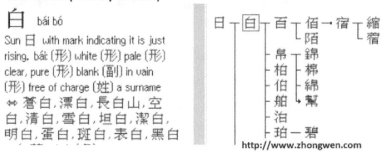

白　bái bó

Sun 日 with mark indicating it is just rising. bái: (形) white (形) pale (形) clear, pure (形) blank (副) in vain (形) free of charge (姓) a surname
↔ 蒼白，漂白，長白山，空白，清白，雪白，坦白，潔白，明白，蛋白，斑白，表白，黑白

http://www.zhongwen.com

Ancient Chinese Character for B

www.artof4elements.com

Ancient Chinese character for B Beo White Bianco Bright Abjad

Symbol B Ancient Chinese character for B Beo White Bianco Bright Abjad Sacred Script of Neolithic Europe and China

Ancient Chinese F (pH) for Father, Egyptians Faraons, Finland, Fenomenalno, Ancient Greek Physics, Philosophy, Flaming FiRe, Funeral (return to God), Flowers, Fjori, Fjur, Fish or FlouR (Food from God)

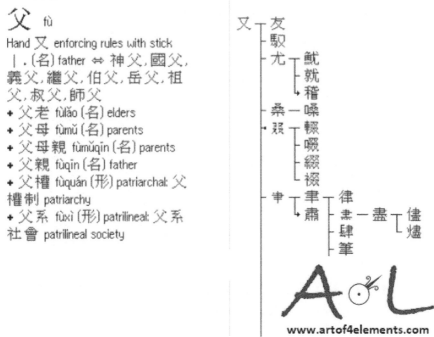

父 fù

Hand 又 enforcing rules with stick

｜.(名) father ⇔ 神父, 國父, 義父, 繼父, 伯父, 岳父, 祖父, 叔父, 師父

+ 父老 fùlǎo (名) elders
+ 父母 fùmǔ (名) parents
+ 父母親 fùmǔqīn (名) parents
+ 父親 fùqīn (名) father
+ 父權 fùquán (形) patriarchal: 父權制 patriarchy
+ 父系 fùxì (形) patrilineal: 父系社會 patrilineal society

www.artof4elements.com

Ancient Chinese character for F as Father

Letter F Ancient Chinese character for F as Father Phenicians Faraons Philosophy Sacred Script of Neolithic Europe and China

One of the earliest ancestors, from this Western side of the planet of our powerful sound F that consists of P+H were Phoenicians and Ancient Greeks some 2,500 BC. As a sacred syllabus it carried the names of Pharaohs, the force of Arabic Phoenicians, the unity of the Family, the dreams of Ferries, Flames of Fire and Flamingos Flight.

It still kept its sacred meaning (hiding the sound of name of God = H) within Facetiae, a Latin word for "cleverness or skillful; Philosophy, Physics, Physic, but it has mapped the Latin for many millennia to be carried war with Ancient Europe, Mediterranean Byzantine Kingdoms carrying now the sound of Phake, accusing the sound PH for any Independent Scientific progress during the last 2,000 years. This motion has unfortunately materialized as a war against Females, that were now turned into Slaves, as supposed to Queens of Ancient Egypt or Goddesses of Ancient Malta.

Ancient Chinese Š Sh Sch 山 in Cirilic

SchopenHoweR ArthuR, ShuBeRT FRanZ, Schumann, SHaKeSpeaR William, Shanti, Shakti, ShiVa, ShankaRa, Shamans, ShanG Dynasty with many KinGs of China, Shanghai

山　shān

Pictograph of mountain peaks. (名)
mountain ⇔ 唐山, 泰山, 長白
山, 嵩山, 冰山, 阿里山, 普
陀山, 衡山, 峨嵋山, 中山,
登山, 火山, 爬山, 玉山, 廬
山, 恆山, 舊金山, 華山
+ 山崩 shānbēng (名) landslide
+ 山川 shānchuān (名) mountains
and streams
+ 山頂 shāndǐng (名) summit
+ 山東 shāndōng (地) Shandong
Province
+ 山洞 shāndòng (名) cave
+ 山風 shānfēng (名) mountain
breeze
+ 山峰 shānfēng (名) mountain peak
+ 山谷 shāngǔ (名) valley
+ 山嶺 shānlǐng (名) mountain range
+ 山麓 shānlù (名) foothill
+ 山脈 shānmài (名) mountain range
+ 山門 shānmén (名) monastery gate
+ 山坡 shānpō (名) mountain slope
+ 山區 shānqū (名) mountain area
+ 山上 shānshàng (名) mountaintop

山─┬ 訕
　├ 舢
　├ 仙
　├ 广 ┬ 岸
　├ 岩 └ 炭 ─ 碳
　└ 崇 岡 崗 峻 嵩 嶼 丞
　嵩 崎 峭 峙 岔 峽 嶺
　峨 密 幽 岊 崛 豈 崖
　豐 峰 屹 嶽 岳 嶄 巍
　崛 嵋 耑 巖 崔 崩 島

www.artof4elements.com

Ancient Chinese character for Š European SH or shui as God divine in human supreme Sacred Script of Neolithic Europe and China

Shen (神) is the Chinese word for god, deity, spirit or theos. A starting

181

point for an understanding of shen is that according to the ancient Chinese, Human is the meeting place of Heaven and Earth. Their number 10 is symbolically depicted as +

In Chinese ancient philosophy yin and yang is a concept of dualism, and we find it mapped within the mystical Jewish Kabbalah and within Hindus sacred texts exploring mantras and meditations. The Ancient Chinese wise or educated men spent lifetimes researching how these seemingly opposite or contrary forces may actually be complementary, and interconnected. Various cultures have translated this wisdom working with the music, symbolism, sounds. While reading any mystical or magical texts, try to go back to the originals, for many a wisdom has been lost in translations and most colorful human intentions.

Ancient Chinese character for X European H or xin meaning mind mental state Heart

Ancient Chinese N, H (Cyrilic), Both in YiN and YaNG, both in oNe & TeN, Noć & NiRVaNa, NorTH (magicaly for the UK representing South), TnejN (MooN day) = Arabic for Monday, BoTH in SuN & MooN

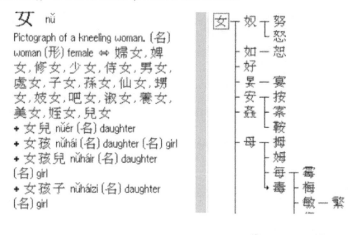

www.artof4elements.com

Ancient Chinese character for N for Nirvana, Night, YiN

Alphabet Symbol N in Ancient Chinese character for N Sacred Script of Neolithic Europe and Ancient China

Ancient Chinese Z, Ž (Z+sacred H), 3 (of Greek + Cyrillic) = ZeN, ZRaK (Slavic for RaY), ZaRaTuSTa, ŽaR (spark of FiRe), ŽuBoR Vode (vs. ŠuM MoRa), ŽiTo, ZeRo, Ancient Greek ZooloGY, ZHonG (name of China = middle) Z+H = Dž, or softer Đ - George, Djavo, JaY, Slavic West - ZaPaD, softer Z = S for Symbol, Slovo, Sacred, Saturn-Day, HaMiS (Saturday in Arabic), ZajR (Arabic small)

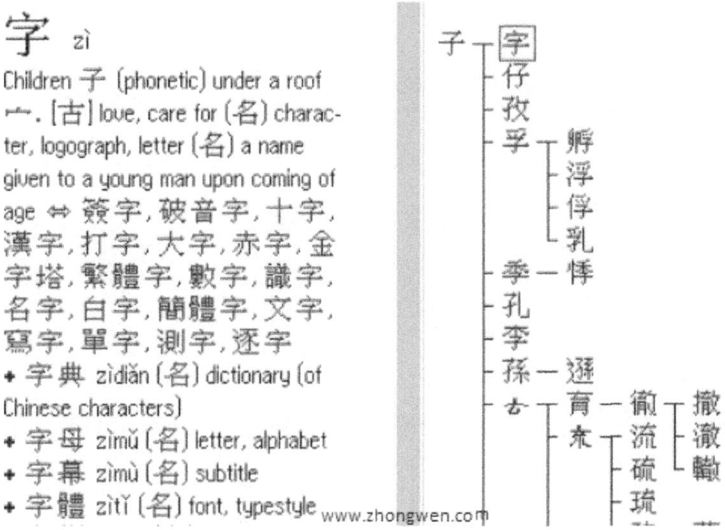

字 zì

Children 子 (phonetic) under a roof ⼧. [古] love, care for (名) character, logograph, letter (名) a name given to a young man upon coming of age ⟷ 簽字, 破音字, 十字, 漢字, 打字, 大字, 赤字, 金字塔, 繁體字, 數字, 識字, 名字, 白字, 簡體字, 文字, 寫字, 單字, 測字, 逐字

◆ 字典 zìdiǎn (名) dictionary (of Chinese characters)

◆ 字母 zìmǔ (名) letter, alphabet

◆ 字幕 zìmù (名) subtitle

◆ 字體 zìtǐ (名) font, typestyle www.zhongwen.com

子 ┬ 字
　 ├ 仔
　 ├ 孜
　 ├ 孚 ┬ 孵
　 │ 　 ├ 浮
　 │ 　 ├ 俘
　 │ 　 └ 乳
　 ├ 季 ─ 悸
　 ├ 孔
　 ├ 李
　 ├ 孫 ─ 遜
　 └ 玄 ┬ 育 ─ 徹 ┬ 撤
　 　 　 └ 充 ┬ 流 └ 澈 ┬ 轍
　 　 　 　 　 ├ 硫
　 　 　 　 　 ├ 琉

A◦L

www.artof4elements.com

Ancient Chinese character for Z as Zen, Zrak, Zdravlje, Zaratusta

Symbol Z in Ancient Chinese character for Z Sacred Script of Neolithic Europe influence of China Zen Zar Zlato

In the begining there was Logos, frequency of that sound was God. Ancient Chinese Y for Y- H- W Y as Chinese for One, Y as YiN or YaNG, YHW symbols & sounds hidden by Priests, Ja, JieN, I (aY), Jedan (Slavic for one), Jovan, JaNuaR, DaY, WaY, PaY, JoaN of aRK, JeRuSaLeM, Jesus, JoHN, JuDaH

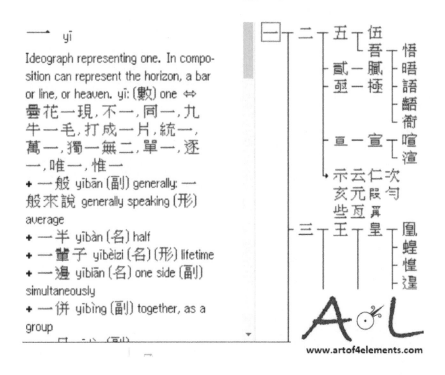

www.artof4elements.com

Yi Chinese character representing One

Yi Chinese character representing One I Io Jahowa Jedan Sacred Script of Neolithic Europe and Influece of China

Ancient Worlds and Sound M

What about M. Within the Eastern philosophical thought M was reserved for Mantra: A word that is sang for God; a vibrational sound found in many forms used to change states of consciousness. It is found in the word of Meditation: meaning a spiritual practice of usually silent prayers known as contemplation, and achieved after concentration. In the late nineteenth century, Theosophists explain "meditation" as a tool used by various spiritual practices drawn from Hinduism, Buddhism, and other Eastern religions. It is found in the word Metaphysics: (Greek

184

meta = beyond and physics = nature). It is found in the word Mind referring to imagination and memory, or within China referring to both thoughts and feelings. We find it in the word Miracle, or Moksha: (Sanskrit मोक्ष Mukti. It also hides Muraqaba: the Sufi word for meditation. Literally meaning "to watch over" and Mysticism: From the Greek mueo "to conceal", a conscious awareness of the divine usually through art and music. In the Hellenistic world, "mystical" referred to secret religious rituals.

Dadiwan, Damaidi from the 5,000 BC

Travelling back in time, even further back, just during the last few decades, our knowledgeable archaeologists, have found a series of inscribed graphs and pictures at Neolitic sites in China, Dadiwan, Damaidi, Banpo (5,000 BC).

Just a word of caution, we at this point have to remind ourselves that we had no writing nor reading whatsoever distributed amongst scholars, unless done by Kings, during the last 2,000 years of our most recent history.

The scripts were considered sacred and were hidden within the monastery walls or Palaces, belonging to the rich.

They were FEW! Before the Age of Enlightenment, in Europe, no books other than Bible could be found in the cities. Pre-electricity, that is just a 100 years ago, 99 % of the people all around our little planet could not read nor write. Holding a 16 century Plato's book in my hands, I could witness how fragile and small books at the time were. So now, when a scientist tells me: 5,000 years BC, I have a deep respect for the archeological findings that is this old. I will not expect an ancient paper copy of the Sunday Times, the finding will be the scripts, symbols carved on the Oracle bones (the shell that is durable for 1,000s of years) or if we are truly lucky, we might hope to find a pottery artefact

Ancient China Dawenkou

An inscription bearing artifacts from the Dawenkou culture, Shandog, are dating to 2800 BC, are from the Longshan culture, descendants of which are the Shang, where the first undisputed Chinese writing appears. At a Dawenkou 陵陽河 大朱村, eighteen isolated pictorial symbols of eight types carved or painted with cinnabar on sixteen pottery jars have been found, excavated from wealthier tombs.

A Chinese Archaeologist, Yu Xingwu hasidentified the circle-and-cloud graph as the Chinese character for "dawn", 旦

Banpo pottery symbols Ancient China 5,000 BC

The symbols found resemble the ancient pictographic script discovered in the Neolithic China so there is no doubt that they can be viewed as the pioneers of primitive writing.

Longshan culture

Eleven characters found on a pottery shard, Longshan culture

The fifth millennium Neolithic village of Banpo, near Xian, China, has yielded pottery vessels incised with signs having striking parallels with the Vinča signs. The 22 different types of rectilinear marks, including

$$\text{Y Ϋ Ѵ Ѵ Х + Ƨ | || ₮ ⊓⊓}$$

are also common Vinča-Tordos signs. Chinese scholars suggest that the signs were used for recording events or quantities and can be considered "precursors of writing".

Banpo signs symbols Ancient China 5000 BC

Comparing various Languages in Neolithic Europe to Understand the development of Sound.

My dear consciousness researchers, the sound resonance on our little planet is supreme. During the Valletta Film Festival, I have a pleasure to see The Hypnotist, a documentary film from Finland, with a story about Master hypnotist Olliver Hawk (1930–1988), who having started his career in Australia, became famous in Finland in the 1960s when hundreds of thousands of people saw Hawk's hypnosis show. His mission in life was within the use of the sacred sounds within his hypnosis work, and he believed that hypnosis was used by the Finish dictator to stay in power and break the democracy, by the army leaders, by the state officials, and that he with his knowledge of the sound frequencies had a profound influence on the political life in Finland.

Symbolism of Flower of Life

A symbolism of Flower of Life has deep spiritual meaning. Its form is a mandala that consists of multiple evenly-spaced, overlapping circles. The Flower of Life pattern is found in ancient spiritual drawings, as the symbol that depicts the evolution of life within the aspects of space and time. Everything has a mathematical pattern. The Flower of Life carries the pattern of the Universal Life Force. The symbol is found carved in stone within the Temple of Osiris at Abydos, Egypt, possibly representing the Eye of Ra, and later in Phoenician, Asian, Middle Eastern, and Christian art. Today famous are Leonardo da Vinci's mystical and occult drawings of the Flower of Life. Understanding The Flower of Life help us understand how the Universe works. This symbol could be used during meditations, or as a protection symbol and some use it to improve the quality of their drinking water.

Jung about Meaning of Mandalas

'Very ancient magical effects are hidden in this symbol for it derives originally from the 'enclosing circle', the 'charmed circle', the magic of which has been preserved in countless folk customs. The image has the obvious purpose of drawing a sulcus primigenius, a magical furrow around the centre, the templum, or temenos (sacred precinct), of the innermost personality, in order to prevent 'flowing out', or to guard by apotropaeic means against deflections through external influences. The magical practices are nothing but the projections of psychic events, which are here applied in reverse to the psyche, like a kind of spell on one's own personality. That is to say, by means of these concrete performances, the attention, or better said, the interest, is brought back to an inner, sacred domain, which is the source and goal of the soul and which contains the unity of life and consciousness. The unity once possessed has been lost, and must now be found again.'

Jung about Mandala, Intro to the Secret of the Golden Flower

Mandala around the fire under stars forming a <3

Love Symbols and Their Meaning

Love knows no boundaries. Symbols of Love connect us to the Force of Love and its Eternal Wisdom.

Heart as a Symbol of Love

We somehow naturally start with the heart as a symbol of love. It was firstly found on coins by the Cyrenes in the 7th century B.C.

It is interesting that the image depicted on the coins was the heart shaped seeds of a plant called Silphium, a type of fennel, that was used as a herbal contraceptive.

The Greeks believed the plant was a gift from Apollo. It was the birth-control medicine of the time so no wonder that its shape became an association for sexuality and love.

The heart shape was most likely first associated with sex, and later with love... One of the first known depiction of a heart as a symbol of romantic love dates back to the 13th century. It is found in a French manuscript where a kneeling lover offers his heart to his lady.

The heart shape is also formed by the heads of two doves in love, an animal associated with Aphrodite, the Greek Goddess of Love.

Doves as a Symbol of Love

Peace Picasso

Doves are considered a symbol of faithful and eternal love because they mate for life. Depictions of two doves together symbolize everlasting love.

Swans as a Symbol of Love

A Swan symbolizes love, grace, purity, and beauty. The swans pair for years, sometimes for a lifetime. The image of two of them swimming creating a shape of a heart is a beautiful universal symbol of love.

Cupid as a Symbol of Love

Cupid or Eros means desire in Greek. Cupid was born out of the chaos alongside his sister Aphrodite. In the Roman Myth he is born from the union of Mars and Venus representing a symbolic merge of Heavenly and Earthly Love. Cupid is often shown as blindfolded symbolizing the love's blindness.

In one tale Cupid as a toddler steals some honey and is stung by bees. He cries and runs to his mother Venus, saying that bees are so small and yet their wounds are very painful. Venus laughs, and tells him that he too is very small, and yet that he delivers the sting of love that can be very painful.

Celtic Love Knot

The Celtic Knot has no beginning and no end, and it stands for the everlasting love.

The symbol represents the perfect union of two people.

When the three knots are laced together,

it symbolizes the Unity of Divine Lovers, God, Man and Woman.

Maple Leaves

In China and Japan the maple leaves are love symbols of the beauty of love in daily life.

Rose

The ancient Greeks and Romans identified the rose with their goddesses of love, Aphrodite and Venus.

Rose represents all things sensual, sacred, pure and romantic. In Rome a wild rose was placed at the entrance door of a house where secret matters were discussed.

Triangle

In Ancient Egypt the Triangle was a symbol of intelligence and it symbolized one's capacity for love. The triangle within the Buddhist Shri Yantra Mandala helps the invocation of love energy.

Rose Quartz

Rose quartz generates strong love energies. This quartz crystal is used to open the heart. Rose quartz is seen as a stone of unconditional love.

Heart Chakra

Within the Yoga Philosophy, Anahata is the 4th chakra, the heart chakra. It is located near the heart. Opening the heart chakra we open to love. Anahata symbolises love, compassion, selflessness and devotion. Anahata's colour is smoke-green-grey.

Its shape is two triangles, creating a star of David that symbolises the union of the masculine and feminine energies. It is often represented by the union of Shiva and Shakti. The chakra's animal is an antelope.

Feng Shui and Love Symbols

The back right corner of any home is the Feng Shui Love and Relationship corner.

In the Feng Shui two of anything represents a harmonious and balanced relationship. The Dragon and Phoenix symbolize a perfect couple.

PHOENIX: A Phoenic dies in its self-made flames to rise again from its own ashes. To alchemists, it symbolizes the destruction and creation of new forms of matter.

SNAKE: A Snake also represents rebirth, male or female sexuality, and fertility. It represents Kundalini that is an Eastern female energy or life-force.

Mandarin Ducks: If separated from its mate, the Mandarin Duck will be devastated. It will yearn for its partner and die from loneliness. Feng Shui suggests that the symbol of Ducks is placed as a pair in the Southwest of a home.

Love Symbols and Hinduism

The ecstasy of devotees that sing hundreds of songs to their Gods embodies the deep feelings of Bhakti and Devotion. Krishna is an important and popular focus of these devotees. Kṛṣṇa in Sanskrit is an adjective meaning 'black' or 'dark'. Krishna is most often depicted as a youthful man with a dark or blue skin playing a flute surrounded with women in ecstasy dancing.

Krishna appears in many forms. When he is together with Radha, he is regarded as supreme lord under the name of Radha-Krishna. Radha is considered to be the perfect devotee. RadhaKrishna cannot be broken into two. Such was the love of Radha towards Krishna that they became one.

Shiva and Shakti as Love Symbols

Shiva is limitless, transcendent, unchanging and formless. He is depicted as a Yogi who lives an ascetic life or as a family man living with his wife Parvati and his two children:

Shakti is a concept of feminine creative power. On the earthly plane, Shakti manifests through fertility.

Chanting of the Sanskrit bij mantra MA is used to call upon the Divine Mother, the Shakti, as well as the Moon.

Shiva is a Tantric couple with Shakti that is energy, movement, action within the existence. Shiva is her transcendent masculine aspect. Shakti manifests in many female forms: Sati, Paravati, Durga, Kali, etc.

Gnostic Cosmology & Archaeology Combined Terms: Universal Music of the Spheres

AdaM

H aDaM Following sacred H through the esoteric studies of our priests, and sacred books, reading it as the Sound of God, we get a beautiful undistorted translation of this phrase to be: H has created D and M. H (as the name of God) creates: D as the Male principle, the YanG of consciousness manifestation, creating sounds of D, TH, G, B or R (Dio, Theo, Bog, Beauty, Ben as Chinese for White, Brahma, God, or Ra) and M as the Female, left, Yin manifestation of the Life force. M that is the first element, water, with Moon as its symbol, symbolically presented as the Eye of Horus in Ancient Egypt. The Bible uses the word אָדָ.ם (X-aDaM) in all of its senses: collectively as the mankind, (Genesis 1:27), gender non-specific as "man and woman" together as in Genesis 5:1-2, as for a male or in the collective sense, and the interplay between the individual "Adam" and the collective "humankind". According to an old Rabbi legend, an angel gave Adam the mysteries and secrets of Kabbalah and of Alchemy, promising that when the human race understand these inspired arts, the curse of the forbidden fruit would be removed and man will again enter into the Garden of Eden.

AUM

The mantra OM is the name of God. Written as A-U-M, it represents the divine energy united in its three aspects: Brahma (creation), Vishnu (preservation) and Shiva (destruction); or Buddhists will relate it to holy body, holy speech and holy mind of Buddha. A Mantra is a word or sound that is repeated, during meditation. Mantras are considered capable of creating transformation of energy / vibration into divine qualities. Mantras are used within various spiritual paths to enhance meditation or to lead to meditation. The Buddha leads us to enlightenment manifesting in the form of the mantra "Om Mani Padme Hum"... It is said that all the teachings of the Buddha are within this mantra. According to Buddhism all beings have the Buddha nature. Your ordinary body, speech and mind are purified and transform into, Buddha's holy body, holy speech and holy mind (symbolically represented by AUM).

Astrology

6,000 B.C. The Sumerians in Mesopotamia note the movements of the planets and stars. 2,400 B.C. The Babylonians (also known as the Chaldeans) have invented the first astrological system with the zodiac wheel that we use today (with planets and houses) around 700 B.C. The oldest known horoscope chart is believed to date to 409 B.C. 331 B.C. Alexander the Great conquers Babylon/Chaldea and the Greeks start making advances in astrology. The modern names for planets and zodiac signs come from Greek literature. In 140 A.C., Ptolemy publishes Tetrabiblos, one of the most revered astrology works ever written. The Arabs continue studying and developing Greek astrology during the Europe's dark ages.

Alexandria

Alexandria is a Mediterranean city in Egypt. During the Hellenistic period, it was so famous to have a lighthouse named among the Seven Wonders of the Ancient World, and a large library visited by many researchers. Founded by Alexander the Great in 331 BC, or chosen by Alexander as his capital city when he settled in Egypt.

Amon Ra

Within the Christian worlds we often use Amin / Alleluia, Buddhists deeply appreciate the sound and frequency of Aum, the ancient Egyptians remind us that the mystical name of God is Amon Ra. Ra or Ta as the sound of the supreme male quality and Ma or Na as the sound of the supreme female quality, these two combining within the name of the Hindhu's supreme God B-Ra-Ma, or Be Ra & Ma. Could it that simple? Perhaps not, but do your-own research further...

The mystical Christians preserved the secret of sound of the supreme God, singing the name Ma-Ri-Ya within a song Ave Marija = mystically equals to Amon-Ra-Yahowa. A typical prayer song both in Judaism and Arabic will praise: Allah, and the Hindus priests when devoting their prayers to their Supreme Male God will sing: Om Namah Siva, or Jay Krishna, or Vishnu Jay, and they have a huge variety of Mantras addressing any sort of Gods. Mystical Buddhists will use "Om Mani Padme Hum", or Hinduist So-Ham Following the name of supreme God, we also came across the frequency of the sounds Xa / Sha / Cha / Ža. Did you know that in Arabic, Ra means "All Seeing" and Ramadan translates as a fast (M of Mangiare) dedicated to God and it is roughly at the same time as Christian Eastern fast. Worshiping Fire our ancestors turned to Ra, creating Sun-days (God's days), CaR was used by Slavs as the title of the King.

Both the ancient Egyptians and Incas remind us that the mystical name of the Sun-Moon God is Amon Ra. Ra or Da as the sounds of the supreme male quality, and Ma or Na as the sounds of the supreme female quality.

Amun

(also Amon, Ammon, Amen, Ancient Egyptian: jmn), was a major ancient Egyptian deity - Amun and his female expression Amaun.et 2,100 BC. Amun was a patron deity of Thebes. Scripts were written about "AM-N", rituals created, history books and trade correspondence, 100s of Canaan letters start with "JMN" salutation. He was the Ancient Egyptian Supreme God with the position of transcendental, self-created creator deity; to the point of monotheism where other gods became manifestations of him. Each manifested as female and male, each carrying a symbol, a letter, a sound. As the chief deity of the Ancient Egyptian Empire, Amun-Ra also came to be worshipped outside Egypt, according to the testimony of ancient Greek historiographers in Libya and Nubia. Rosetta Stone's hydrographic sacred script identifies it as NΘR manifesting as nXr, nÐr, nČr, etc. In Ancient Greece he was identified with Zeus. ΘΕΟΣ (θεὸς or Δίὸς) or Dios of the Catholic Roman Church.

Ancient Egypt

Ancient Egypt was a civilization of ancient North Africa, concentrated along the Nile River. WSIR Land of Isis, Ancient Egypt. 3000 BC Kingdoms of Upper and Lower Egypt unite. Successive dynasties witness flourishing trade, prosperity and the development of great cultural traditions. Writing, including hieroglyphics, is used as an instrument of state. Schools and trade flourish, mathematics, art, rituals... Construction of the pyramids - around 2,500 BC - is an amazing architectural achievement. 332 BC - Alexander the Great, of ancient Macedonia, founds Alexandria. A Macedonian dynasty rules until 31 BC. 1517 - Egypt absorbed into the Turkish Ottoman Empire. 1798 - Napoleon Bonaparte sails to Egypt.

Athena

Athena Ἀθηνᾶ was the Ancient Greek Goddess, the daughter of Zeus. She sprang from Zeus's head, fully-grown. She was Zeus's favorite child. **Belief in One God in ancient Egypt and AXeN.**

The solitary sun-god in the reign of king AXenaten. We know of him, for he has left us with 350 letters carved in 1,350 BC, currently known as "Canaan or Amarna Letters" from the time of the Babylon Kingdom sent by the Ancient Egyptian Pharaoh AXeNaTeN/M during his reign 1,350 BC to 1,330 BC, to his Rulers around the country. Canaan is also known as Phoenicia or present day Lebanon, Syria, Jordan, and Israel. From the King to his Knights! Can you get the complexity and the beauty of this task! What an advanced culture to communicate with carved letters! Pharao Akhenaten (aXeNaTeN) and his wife Nefertiti ruled there. The city covered an area of approximately 12 km; on the west bank of Nile, and the land was set aside to provide crops for the city's population. The entire city was encircled with a total of 14 boundary stele. The tribe that lived in the region and founded a few settlements, including Babylon, was called Akh.et-aten aXeN Their worshiped Sun Goddess called Axen.

Osiris

The cult of Ancient Egyptian god Osiris passed to us the myth of the Egyptian Resurrection. The Egyptian death ritual is fully historically documented. The most famous text of The Egyptian Book of the Dead is the Papyrus of Ani, by the priest Ani of Thebes in 1,250 BC, providing instructions to help the dead soul face Gods in the afterlife.

WSR The name of Egypt = tells us the Ancient Egyptian Kings is WSIR, the Land of Osiris, god of the dead, or "diseased" since the belief was that soul doesn't die. His female form takes the name of ISIS.

Ancient Egyptians have introduced a belief in resurrection, with life after death, so "becoming Osiris" or re-incarnating through Holy Spirit symbolically represented as aNX (cross).

Writing was believed to have been given to humanity by the Egyptian god Thoth Thōth (Θώθ). The items always found in the tombs are the ancient Egyptian funerary texts. The text incorporates the ancient Egyptian Book of the Dead as early as 3000 BC. The Ancient Egyptian Negative Confessions are the Ten Commandments of Jewish and Christian ethics, later perceived as divine revelation.

Aristotle

Aristotle (384 BC - 322 BC) was an ancient Greek philosopher. Aristotle was born on the Chalcidic peninsula of Macedonia, in northern Greece. His father, Nicomachus, was the physician of the King Amyntas III (393 BC - 370 BC), and grandfather of Alexander the Great. After his father's death Aristotle migrated to Athens, where he joined the Academy of Plato (428 - 348 BC). Best known as the teacher of Alexander the Great, he was the author of the philosophical and scientific system that became the framework for both Christian and Islamic philosophy.

Aristotelian concepts remained embedded in Western thinking all through the Renaissance, and the Age of Enlightenment. "Everyone must do philosophy, Aristotle claims. The best form of philosophy is the contemplation of the universe of nature; it is for this purpose that God made human beings. All else—strength, beauty, power, and honour—is worthless."

According to Aristotle, 'εὐδαιμονία' (wellbeing or long-term happiness) is achieved when during the life-time a human being achieves health, wealth, knowledge, friends and this in turn leads to the perfection of human nature.

Amarna

Amarna or Tell el-Amarna is today an Egyptian archaeological site with the remains of the capital city established and built by the Pharaoh Akhenaten, in 1346 BC in the Upper Ancient Egypt. The Horizon of Aton or AΘeN or AXeN devoted to the Sun Goddess, one and only, that became famous for the Pharaoh's 100s of carved in stone Amarna Letters sent to his Kingdom, announcing the religious reform.

Aphrodites aFRoDiTeS

Aphrodite is an ancient Greek Love Goddess. She was identified with the Roman goddess Venus. Aphrodite's major symbols include myrtles, roses, doves, sparrows, and swans. Aphrodite's main cult centers were Cythera, Cyprus, Corinth, and Athens. Her main festival was the Aphrodisia, which was celebrated annually in midsummer. The cult of Aphrodite in Cyprus, was centred in the Paphos area and dates from 1,500 BC. The birthplace of Aphrodite is at Cyprus town Petra Tou Romiou. In the legend Aphrodite emerged from the sea foam and became consort of king Kinyras. The Terracotta Astarte female figure with large pierced ears and hands below her breasts, and head of an animal 1450-1200 BC in British Museum, speaks of the Assyrian goddess Astarte / Ishtar. The cult of Aphrodite may date back further to the Assyrian cults of Ishtar and Astarte. There is evidence that Ishtar Astarte were worshiped in Cyprus brought to the island by the Phoenicians, along with the Egyptian cult of Hathor, who may also have been identified with Aphrodite.

APHRODITE was the Olympian goddess of love, beauty, pleasure and procreation. According to Plato, there are two Aphrodites, "the elder, having no mother, who is called the heavenly Aphrodite—she is the daughter of Uranus; the younger, who is the daughter of Zeus and Dione—her we call common." She was depicted as a beautiful woman often accompanied by the winged godling Eros (Love). Her attributes included a dove, apple, scallop shell and mirror. In classical sculpture and fresco she was usually depicted nude. She was syncretized with the Roman goddess Venus. Parents: In the Iliad: Zeus and Dione; her Mesopotamian equivalent is: Inanna or Ishtar. Aphrodite Urania (Ancient Greek: Ἀφροδίτη Οὐρανία) was an epithet of the Greek goddess Aphrodite, signifying "heavenly" or "spiritual". According to Herodotus, the Arabs called this aspect of the goddess "Alitta" or "Alilat" (Ἀλίττα or Ἀλιλάτ).

Babylon

Babylon was the capital city of Babylonia, a kingdom in ancient Mesopotamia, now Iraq, between the 1800 and 600 BC. It was built along both banks of the Euphrates river. Writing was believed to have been given to humanity by the Egyptian god Thoth Thōth (Θώθ). In 1887, a local Egyptian woman has uncovered a cache of over 350 stone carved tablets written in cuneiform. The Amarna Letters from the Ancient Egyptian King Tut-ankh-amun were discussing legal matters and the religious reform dedicated to the AΘen: to Babylonia, to Assyria, to Mittani, to Arzawa, Alashia and Hatti. Today, these most ancient, carved in stone booklets are scattered in the museums all over the world. Just for the history lovers, the timing does correspond to the timing of Moshe's 10 commandments (around 1400 BC). Several letters date back to the rule of Akhenaten's father, Amenhotep III (1390 – 1353 BC), were among those found at Amarna.

Balkans

The Balkans have been inhabited since the Paleolithic, and the Neolithic entered Europe through the Balkan peninsula. The Bronze and Iron Ages were fully developed following the Danube river by the sophisticate city states and within the Mediterranean region by Ancient Greeks, who controlled the eastern part of the Mediterranean. The comparison of genetic distances among the different Aromun groups and their surrounding neighbors, when using mtDNA sequences, revealed great genetic homogeneity in the Balkan peninsula and in particular no significant differences (P < 0.05) among Greeks, Italians, Romanians and Bulgarians or Macedonians, read Slavs of the region, including Serbs, Croats, B-H, Montenegro, Slovenia. Now, who were the Barbarians at the time? What does DNA analysis say about Slavs on Balkan? Serbs have almost 1/3 of the Balkan origin gene which peaks in Herzegovina. It has originated in Balkan and spread out 7000 years ago and into other people now called Slavs (in Europe). However, it is not the most prevalent for the other Slavs - only certain South Slavs, like Serbs, Macedonians, Montenegrins, Bosniaks & Bosnian Serbs and Southern Croats.

Belgrade

Belgrade (Serbian: Beograd / Београд, or 'White City' is the capital and largest city of Serbia. It is located at the confluence of the Sava and Danube rivers and the crossroads of the Pannonian Plain and the Balkan Peninsula. One of the most important prehistoric cultures of Europe, the Vinča culture, evolved within the Belgrade area in the 6th millennium BC. In antiquity, Thraco-Dacians inhabited the region and, after 279 BC, Celts settled the city, naming it Singidūn.

It was conquered by the Romans under the reign of Augustus and awarded Roman city rights in the mid-2nd century. It was settled by the Slavs in the 520s, and changed hands several times between the Byzantine Empire, the Frankish Empire, the Bulgarian Empire, and the Kingdom of Hungary before it became the seat of the Serbian king

Stefan Dragutin in 1284. It frequently passed from Ottoman to Habsburg rule, which saw the destruction of most of the city during the Austro-Ottoman wars. In the period after the Serbian Revolution, Belgrade was again named the capital of Serbia in 1841.

Byzantine Empire

The Byzantine Empire, also referred to as the Eastern Roman Empire, or Byzantium, was the continuation of the Roman Empire in its eastern provinces during Late Antiquity and the Middle Ages, when its capital city was Constantinople (modern Istanbul, formerly Byzantium). Founded: 330 AC, Dissolved: 1453 AC. Between 324 and 330, Constantine I (306–337 AC) who was from Niš, today's Serbia, has transferred the main capital of the Roman Empire from Rome to Byzantium, later known as Constantinople ("City of Constantine"). Christianity became the Empire's official state religion.

Buddha

The Buddha (500 to 400 BC), born in Nepal, was a philosopher, mendicant, meditator, spiritual teacher, and religious leader who lived in Ancient India. He is revered as the founder of the world religion of Buddhism, and worshipped by most Buddhist schools as the Enlightened One who has transcended Karma and escaped the cycle of birth and rebirth.

Within Buddhism, prayer is seen as a powerful spiritual practice that enhances meditation.

„Universally wishing sentient beings, Friends, foes, and karmic creditors, all to activate the bodhi mind, and all to be reborn in the Pure Land of Ultimate Bliss.' 願以此功德 莊嚴佛淨土 上報四重恩 下濟三途苦 普願諸眾生 冤親諸債主 悉發菩提心 同生極樂國

Danube

The Danube is Europe's second-longest river, after the Volga. It is located in Central and Eastern Europe. German Donau, Slovak Dunaj, Hungarian Duna, Serbo-Croatian and Bulgarian Dunav, Romanian Dunărea, Ukrainian Dunay. Ister, equivalent to the Ancient Greek "Ἴστρος", also meant the Danube. The people of the Vinča (Serbia) - Danube civilisation lived in permanent settlements of hundreds to a few thousands of houses since 9,000 years ago – 6,000 BC. The archeological evidence for Old European civilization consists of houses, ceramics, copper implements, figurines, shells, and graves dating back to 5,000 BC - 3,000 BC. Located in Serbia and Romania, around the Danube river bank, we find villages and proto-cities enlightening us about the Ancient Europe's Copper Age. The overwhelming majority of the excavated female statues, found with inscription and inside the graves, speak of the Old European society as matriarchal. The ceramics and metallurgy and the trade was well developed.

Dios

Pulsation, vibration, rhythm exists everywhere as Akasha / Sound / Waves and we hope to reach the vibration of Wisdom embedded Logic or Love Enlightened Intelligence transcending our microcosmic limitations understanding the macrocosms. When asked Do you believe in God? in a Q&A interview with Malta Today, Nataša Pantović answered "As a dynamic, Orphic, hermaphrodite Universe of Consciousness, Yin and Yang manifestations... then yes."

Diana

Diana is the daughter of Jupiter and the Titan Leto. The Seikilos score Ancient Greek Epitaph of Seikilos lyrics and ancient musical score 100 AC, we find her name written as ΕΝΘΑ In Greek mythology, Dia-Na was called Artemis.

Diana is a goddess in Roman and Hellenistic religion. People regard Diana and the moon as one and the same. Diana was venerated as a triple goddess beginning in the late 600 BC, Diana as huntress, Diana as the moon, Diana of the underworld. ΘaNa

Based on the earlier writings of Plato, the Neoplatonist philosophers considered Diana to be one of the primary animating, or life-giving, deities. Proclus, citing Orphic tradition, concludes that Diana "extends these genitals, distributing as far as to subterranean natures the prolific power of [Bacchus]." Within the oldest ever Ancient Greek musical composition / liturgy,

Orphism

Orpheus, the Thracian's musician god, according to legend was a disciple of Dionysus, but had argued against practices of orgies in the name of Apollo, the god of reason. He was murder by the maenads, the female followers of Dionysus. Orpheus death was considered a sacrifice to redeem mankind for its sins.

Some archaeologists believe that Orpheus could have been a real person who resided in the Rhodope Mountains, a Dionysian priest, an initiate of Egyptian mysteries. His cult proclaimed asceticism, was against sacrifice, and taught the transmigration of souls. His followers, including Pythagoras, Plato, Aristotle and Alexander speak of the soul's capacity to experience the divine. The initiated students had learned to break free, resurrect and experience happiness in the afterlife.

Dionysus

In his religion, identical with or closely related to Orphism, Dionysus was believed to have been born from the union of Zeus and Persephone, and to have himself represented a chthonic or underworld aspect of Zeus. Dionysus was the ancient Greek god of wine, winemaking, grape cultivation, fertility, ritual madness, theater, and religious ecstasy. His Roman name was Bacchus. He may have been worshiped as early as 1500-11000 BC by Mycenean Greeks. Gamzigrad is an archaeological site, spa resort and UNESCO World Heritage Site of Serbia, The entrance is ornamented with a luxurious mosaic with the image of the Greek god Dionysus.

The Derveni papyrus (500 BC) is an ancient Macedonian papyrus that was found in 1962, and was finally published, just recently, in 2006. It is a philosophical treatise written as a commentary on an Orphic poem, a theogony concerning the birth of the gods, compiled in the circle of the philosopher AnaXagoras. Derveni Papyrus, at Thesaloniki Museum, Greece, 340 BC and Orphism The roll itself dates to around 340 BC, during the reign of Philip II of Macedon, making it Europe's oldest surviving manuscript.

Dionysus was the ancient Greek god of wine, fertility, theater, and religious ecstasy. His Roman name was Bacchus (Ba-Ču-S). Worshiped as early as 1,500 BC by Mycenean Greeks, in the area of Ancient Balkan. The village Gamzigrad, 200 AC, is at the banks of the Crni Timok River in Serbia, has the remains of Romula's villa called Felix Romuliana, the memorial of Galerius, co-ruler of Diocletian and Constantine. The most amazing complex consists of a palace, a number of temples, and the sacred burial site, was dedicated to Ancient Greek Dionysus, and the Emperor and his mother Romula, who after their death were ritualistically blessed to become post mortal gods, goddess Romula, by the consecration act at the near-by mount Magura. "The mosaic representation of Dionysus and the wall relief depicting a sleeping Ariadne symbolize the idea of death – and resurrection. The Gamzigrad depiction of Dionysus is the visual representation of this god's permanent aspiration to bring humans into the world of gods after making them immortal. Dionysus is the savior of souls and the one who bestows eternal life." the Serbian Archeologist Maja Živić, says about Felix Romuliana

Divine

Pythagoras symbolize Cosmos: as the number 1 that is Unity or Monad, a point.

Death

...death is an important interest, especially to an aging person. A categorical question is being put to him, and he is under an obligation to answer it. To this end he ought to have a myth about death, for reason shows him nothing but the dark pit into which he is descending. Myth, however, can conjure up other images for him, helpful and enriching pictures of life in the land of the dead." Jung (1959) about Archetype, the myth of Dying Answering the question why the focus on death, the ancient age-old heritage of humanity: an archetype, is rich of examples: Ancient Serbia, Ancient Greece, Ancient Malta, Ancient Cypriot. The Tibetans have further elaborated the "art" of dying well, within their ancient text: the Tibetan book of Living and Dying. Back in time, when our ancestors' focus was mainly Death, the cult of Ancient Egyptian god Osiris passed to us the myth of the Egyptian Resurrection. The essence of the Egyptian death ritual is fully historically documented. The most famous text of The Egyptian Book of the Dead is the Papyrus of Ani, by the priest Ani of Thebes in 1,250 BC, providing instructions to help the soul face the Gods in the afterlife.

Ethiopia

Ethiopia, the country was once historically known as Abyssinia. Menelik I founded the Ethiopian empire in the 1000 BC. Ethiopia is the oldest independent country in Africa and one of the most ancient nation in the world. Under King Ezana, Aksum was converted (400 AC) to Christianity. Many historians agree that Ethiopia is one of the oldest countries in the world. While we know that human life has existed in Ethiopia for millions of years thanks to skeletal fragments uncovered, it's generally agreed that Ethiopia developed as a country in 980 BC. According to every major ancient Greek historian, and as written and recorded in their testimony, the kingdom of ancient Ethiopia is older than ancient Egypt. Jesus spoke Aramaic. Aramaic is an ancient language that has since evolved into several languages spoken in the Middle East. Amharic is spoken mostly in and around Ethiopia, where it's the national language. The city of Aksum likely formed around 400 BC. Legend has it that the kingdom was first established by the son of King Solomon of Israel and the Queen of Sheba of Ethiopia. Aksum began to rise in power around 100 AC.

When in Ethiopia helping Sister Ludgarda within her 150 kids orphanage, wondering the streets of Addis, I've learned that Constantine the Great (272-337 AC) born in Nish (today's Serbia) was not the first King to introduce Christianity to his Empire, Constantinople, later Istanbul. Ethiopians have done it just a few years before him leaving the historians and two countries to fight for the right to be called First to this very day. The earliest found gospels of John, found in Egypt, date back to this time. In an ancient monastery in Northern Ethiopia archaeologists have discovered Biblical scripts carbon dated in Oxford to be around 400 AC.

A Syrian monk apparently settled in Ethiopia in the year 494 AC bringing the scripts with him. The texts were written in Geez, the ancient language predating Ethiopia's Amharic. One of the official languages of the region was also Ancient Greek, for it was in Athens that we had the schools and the tradition of writing manuscripts. The Egyptian was written in two scripts – using symbols and using script.

Eros

Eros – In Greek mythology, the personification of love, a cosmogonic force of nature; psychologically, the function of relationship. "Woman's consciousness is characterized more by the connective quality of Eros than by the discrimination and cognition associated with Logos. In men, Eros ... is usually less developed than Logos. In women, on the other hand, Eros is an expression of their true nature..." C. Jung "Anima and Animus".

Gaia

Gaia (Ancient Greek: Γαῖα), is the personification of the Earth in Greek mythology. She was a primordial being, one of the first to have sprung forth from the void of Chaos. Back in time, the civilization of Babylon, as we know it, lasted from about 2350 to 1595 BC, later ruled by the Hittites. Assyria lasted from 1900 BC to 650 AC. Much of what we know about Mesopotamian mythology comes from Amarna tablets.

The Greek myths we research from the pottery artifacts and 1 book known as Theogony Θεογονία "Birth of the Gods" by Hesiod 700 BC.

Unfortunately, world has passed through 2,000 years of "only Religious texts" as reading materials and a huge distraction of art & culture during 1st and 2nd world war. However, we do have a pretty clear picture of the gods / goddesses of the Mesopotamian pantheon.

Apsu, not technically a god, first emerged out of chaos. Tiamat (Ti Mati in Slavic), a goddess is depicted as a beautiful woman, the mother of gods. When she turned against the gods she became depicted as a dragon-like monster. Bel-Marduk, as the patron god of Babylon, killed Tiamat and used 1/2 of her body to create the sky, and the other 1/2 to create the land. He used the blood of Tiamat's favored warrior to create humans.

A bit like Titans of Greeks.

God

The philosophical research concerning the divine and consciousness poses the question: Is there a meaning / sense / purpose to voicing / writing / reading as us "finite beings" talk about God and Infinity? Is a human being really able to discuss God and Cosmos? Mostly resonating with the Neo-Platonic definition of God, viewing God as a mathematical symbol, Pythagoras gave the name of Monad (1) to god, and Dyad (2) to matter. The Monad (indescribable) emanated the Demiurge (Tao, Consciousness, or a Transcendent Source) or the creator. Plato, in the Socratic dialogue Timaeus, refers to Demiurge as a benevolent force that has created the world out of Chaos. Plotinus metaphorically identified the Demiurge as the Greek God Zeus (θεὸς)

Plotinus who is noted as the founder of Neoplatonism metaphorically identified the Demiurge as the Greek God Zeus. Aristotle equated matter with the formation of the elements moved to action by force or motion. These two are known as Aristotle's Energeia and Plato's

Demiurge. The Demiurge of Neoplatonism is the Nous (mind of God), and it is: 1. Arche – "beginning" or the source of all things, 2. Logos – "reason" or the cause behind all, 3. Harmonia – "harmony" reflected with the Numbers in mathematics Zeus of the Greeks (θεὸς or Δίὸς) or Dios of the Catholic Roman Church.

Goddess

Mathematics is described as the science of pattern and music as the art of pattern, both using meditation within the process of contemplation developing own language of symbols.

We find Ancient Egyptian name of God to be: NΘR (nTr) resonating pretty well with the Bible's creation myth: H aDaM or the Ancient Chinese Taoist Tao Te Ching story of Yi (as one) that has created aR (as two) and SaN (as three), all talk about the same Theological concept of Trinity of sounds and frequencies that have carried the manifestation into Being, as female and male.

Reading the demotic script, our oldest recorded script of the Golden rulers of the Mediterranean region, we read the name of Divine to be -

NΘR = T (within the Rosetta Stone) was translated in Ancient Greek as Theo or the symbol Θ. Pronounced as Č or X or Sh or DŽ symbolically represented as a snake or a spiral, has created Na and Ra.

Na = Gold, to die, underworld, moon, a female sound is the name used by Babylon NeBo or NuT

Ra = sun, light, FiRe, a male sound

Ancient Greeks use θεα for "goddess" and Zeus of Greeks (Babylon's Jupiter or Bel-Marduk) is θεὸς or Δίὸς and Dios of the Catholic Roman Church.

Reading the demotic script, our oldest recorded script of the Golden rulers of the Mediterranean region, we read the name of Divine to be -

214

nTr = ΦΘΑ or ΘΕΟΣ or ΘΕΟΥ or ΘΕΟΥΣ as GoD or BRaMa or AmonRa or LoGoS = read as nΘr with Θ pronounced as T, X, Th or nDr pronounced as nÐr

NΘR = T (within the Rosetta Stone) was translated in Ancient Greek as Theo or the symbol Θ. Pronounced as Č or X or Sh or DŽ symbolically represented as a snake or a spiral, has created Na and Ra

Gods

In Chinese ancient philosophy yin and yang is a concept of dualism, and we find it mapped within the mystical Jewish Kabbalah and within Hindus sacred texts exploring mantras and meditations. The Ancient Chinese wise or educated men spent the lifetimes researching how these seemingly opposite or contrary forces may actually be complementary, and interconnected. Various cultures have translated this wisdom working with the music, symbolism, sounds. While reading any mystical or magical texts, try to go back to the originals, for many a wisdom has been lost in translations and most colorful human intentions. For example, Ancient Chinese character for Š European SH or shui as God Shen (神) is the Chinese word for god, deity, spirit or theos. A starting point for an understanding of shen is that according to the ancient Chinese, Human is the meeting place of Heaven and Earth.

The number 10 is symbolically depicted as + within the development of sounds, symbols of Ancient Greece, Ancient Europe, Ancient China.

Gold

A symbol of Ancient Egyptian Horus „ON".

Symbolically represented as "O" the Egyptian Hrw, Horus was adopted into ancient Greek as Ὧρος, Hōros, a mountain, gold. Gold was the representation of „0" or Ὦ". This is the „0" of Ancient Greeks.

Golden Ratio

In geometry, a golden spiral is a logarithmic spiral whose growth factor is φ, the golden ratio. Golden ratio refers to the Fibonacci Sequence (0, 1, 1, 2, 3, 5, 8, 13, ...) , in which each term is the sum of the previous... The mathematical ideas the Fibonacci sequence leads to, the golden ratio, spirals and similar curves. The number phi, often known as the golden ratio, is a mathematical concept that people have known about since the time of the ancient Greeks. It is an irrational number and goes on forever after the decimal point. The golden ratio describes predictable patterns on everything from atoms to huge stars in the sky. The ratio is derived from something called the Fibonacci sequence, named after its Italian founder, Leonardo Fibonacci. Nature uses this ratio to maintain balance, and the financial markets seem to as well.

Greece

The name of Greece Hellas or Hellada (Greek: Ελλάς, Ελλάδα),.in the Old Testament, is used for the Hebrew word Javan, which is equivalent to Ionia, that includes not only Greece but western Asia Minor. In the New Testament, Greece is called Hellas, a name supposed to have belonged first to a single city, but at length applied to the whole country south of Macedonia. about 146 BC. The Romans conquered Greece, and afterwards organized two great provinces, namely, Macedonia, and Achaia. The country was bounded north by Macedonia and Illyricum, from which it was separated by mountains, south by the Mediterranean sea, east by the Aegean sea, and west by the Ionian sea. It was generally known under the three great divisions of Peloponnesus, Hellas, and Northern Greece. Peloponnesus, was the southern peninsula; it included the famous cities, Sparta, Corinth, Crete. Greeks immigrated to Egypt after Alexander the Great overran Egypt, Syria, and the East. The seat of government moved from Rome to Constantinople, in 350 AC, transferring the ruler ship of the Roman Empire to the Grecian districts.

Yi Ching

The I Ching or Yi Jing, usually translated as Book of Changes or Classic of Changes, is an ancient Chinese divination text and among the oldest of the Chinese classics. The Ancient Chinese Yi Jing starts with the hexagrams Qian and Kun. Qian is heaven and Kun is earth. The Bagua are eight symbols used in Taoist cosmology to represent the fundamental principles of reality, seen as a range of eight interrelated concepts. Each consists of three lines, each line either "broken" or "unbroken", respectively representing yin or yang, 0 or 1 forming binary numbers 000-111. Hexagram 1 is named 乾 (qián), "Force". Other variations include "the creative", "strong action", "the key", and "god". Its inner (lower) trigram is ☰ (乾 qián) force = (天) heaven, and its outer (upper) trigram is the same. Tiān (天) is one of the oldest Chinese terms for heaven and a key concept in Chinese mythology, philosophy, and religion. During the Shang dynasty, the Chinese referred to their supreme god as Shàngdì or Dì (帝,"Lord").

Yoga

Yoga is a group of physical, mental, and spiritual practices or disciplines which originated in ancient India. There is a broad variety of yoga schools, in Hinduism, Buddhism, and Jainism. "Yoga as a system of knowledge went into many details about how energies within our spines interact with the brain, involving drawings (mandalas), sounds (mantras), symbols (within each of 7 chakra). Yoga examines how the various physical, mental or emotional dirt within the body creates emotional blockages. Mastering concentration, meditation or breath, brings both: prolonging life or attaining what Yogis call enlightenment. Yoga has developed some interesting "solder-like" practices for the improvement of Willpower.

Horus

In Egyptian mythology Horus was the god of light, element of AiR, often depicted as a man with the head of a Bird, falcon. Being the element of Air, Horus is the sky, his images have the sun as his right eye and the moon as his left. The sound frequency and the use of symbols within our mystical spiritual traditions, all through the centuries of our existence on this planet, carried the initiation into the altered states of consciousness, our (H}ope to transmit the spiritual energy between various levels of reality. A symbol of Ancient Egyptian Horus is „ON".

Our 1st "O" the Egyptian Hrw, Horus was adopted into ancient Greek as Ὧρος, Hōros, a Mountain, gold. Gold represented as „0" or Ὧ".

Logos

Plotinus in interpreting Logos as the principle of meditation, gives methods to achieve ecstasy using Logos as the Divine Eternal Principle existing as the interrelationship between the Soul, the Spirit (nous), and the One. For Plotinus, the relationship between the three by the outpouring of Logos from the higher principle to the Soul, or by eros (loving) coming from the lower principle. Centuries later, Carl Jung contrasted logos vs eros represented as the alchemical Sol and Luna, science and mysticism, or conscious and unconscious. All other Gods are born as frequencies, sounds, symbols as 22 consonants of the alphabet.

Mount Sinay

Jabal, ShaRa or Sinai Mountain was always considered particularly sacred JaBaL Ideid, which Emmanuel Anati has excavated, dates back to 2350 – 2000 BC. was a major Palaeolithic cult centre, with the surrounding plateau covered with art, shrines, altars, stone circles, paved with over 40,000 rock engravings. Mount Sinai traditionally known as Jabal is a mountain in the Sinai Peninsula of Egypt that is a location of the biblical Mount Sinai of Moses. The word for moon is "S-N", a Babylonia SiN. Immediately north of the mountain is the 6th century Saint Catherine's Monastery. The summit has a mosque that is still used by Muslims, and a Greek Orthodox chapel, constructed in 1934 on the ruins of a 16th-century church, that is not open to the public. The chapel encloses the rock which is considered to be the source for the biblical Tablets of Stone. At the summit also is "Moses' cave", where Moses was said to have waited to receive the Ten Commandments.

Similarly The Song of Deborah, which textual scholars consider to be one of the oldest parts of the bible, suggests that Yahweh dwelt at the Mount Sha-Ra, Mount Sinai, a sacred place dedicated to SHa. In the Biblical account, God was accompanied by divine sounds coming from heaven, sound of female and male voices that have already been on this holy mountain. In the classical rabbinical literature, "Mount Sinai" became synonymous with holiness, and the record tells us that the peaks "sang a chorus of praise to God", heard by El-aY-SHa, the prophet from the story of Moses (MoSHe) hearing:

"This is my name forever, the name you shall call me, from generation to generation." and has sent them "into the land of the Canaanites, Hittites, Amorites, Perizzites, Hivites and Jebusites – the land flowing with milk and honey.' Y or I am – H – W (vatra - fire) were the sounds given, as the vibrations of the Supreme.

Nature

"Materializing within a body we call our own Self / Atman / Unit consciousness within a country or family we call own, we inherit the cultural unconscious set-up, yet with no physical memory of the accumulated progress of our collective society's story.

A UN report tells us that 1,000,000 species are to be extinct during the next few decades, more than the number of living beings extinct through 1,000s of years of evolution. What do you think of that?!!

After we incarnate on this little planet, we take decades of schooling to develop fairly low level memory of the intrinsic matter, and we are left guessing properties of the primordial / spiritual matter.

Our parents' circumstances, family history, relationships with the friends or enemies, our priests, teachers, journalists, contribute to our conscious and subconscious leanings. Whether we like it or not, the strongest physical mechanisms within our emotional or a mental body is the hormonal or chemical input our brain receives, as part of our survival instincts." Nataša Pantović. The Power of Nature is further researched in the Novel Tree of Life and its applied aspects within the Conscious Creativity.

Nadhi

Nāḍī (Sanskrit: नाड़ी, lit. a 'tube' is a term for the channels through which, in traditional Indian medicine and spiritual knowledge, the energies such as prana of the physical body, the subtle body and the causal body are said to flow. Within this philosophical framework, the nadis are said to connect at special points of intensity, forming 7 chakras. The three principal nadis run from the base of the spine to the head, and are the ida on the left, the sushumna in the centre, and the pingala on the right. The nadis play a role in yoga, as many yogic practices, mudras and pranayama, are intended to open and unblock the nadis. The ultimate aim of some yogic practises are to direct prana into the sushumna nadi enabling kundalini to rise, and thus bring about moksha, or liberation.

Middle Ages or Medieval Period

In the history of Europe, the Middle Ages or Medieval Period lasted from the 5th to the late 15th century. After Ancient Greek's fall, European history has taken a turn towards "darkness" that has lasted until the Renaissance and the Age of Discovery or the Age of Colonializations that for the Colonized countries became "darkness" and for the Colonizing Powers became a huge source of income through the unfair trade of slaves, gold, raw materials, silk, coffee, tea, etc.. The Middle Ages saw North Africa and the Middle East, once part of the Byzantine Empire, came under the rule of the Islamic empire. The still sizeable Byzantine Empire, Rome's or Ancient Greek's direct continuation, survived in the Eastern Mediterranean (Balkan countries) and remained a major power. The empire's law code, the Corpus Juris Civilis or "Code of Justinian", was rediscovered in Northern Italy in the 11th century. Monasteries were founded as campaigns to Christianize pagan Europe. The Kings were served by their mostly feudal population (99%) and all the learnings became either Court or Church based.

Mars

The oldest cuneiform literature of Babylonians divide the fixed stars into three groups: th e stars of Anu, Enlil and Ea. Of the planets five were recognized: Jupiter, Venus, Saturn, Mercury and Mars. These five planets were identified with the gods of the Babylonian pantheon In Greek mythology, Persephone (pər-SEF-ə-nee; Greek: Περσεφόνη), also called Kore (KOR-ee; Greek: Κόρη; "the maiden"), is the daughter of Zeus and Demeter. She became the queen of the underworld through her abduction by Hades, the god of the underworld. The myth of her abduction represents her function as the personification of vegetation, which shoots forth in spring and withdraws into the earth after harvest; hence, she is also associated with spring as well as the fertility of vegetation. Similar myths appear in the cults of male gods like Attis, Adonis, and Osiris, and in Minoan Crete. Persephone as a vegetation goddess and her mother Demeter were the central figures of the Eleusinian Mysteries, which promised the initiated a more enjoyable prospect after death. In some versions, Persephone is the mother of Zeus' son Dionysus, (or Iacchus, and/or Zagreus, as a result of their identification with Dionysus). The origins of her cult are uncertain, but it was based on ancient agrarian cults of agricultural communities. Persephone was commonly worshipped along with Demeter and with the same mysteries. To her alone were dedicated the mysteries celebrated at Athens in the month of Anthesterion. In Classical Greek art, Persephone is invariably portrayed robed, often carrying a sheaf of grain. She may appear as a mystical divinity with a sceptre and a little box, but she was mostly represented in the process of being carried off by Hades. Her name has numerous historical variants. These include Persephassa (Περσεφάσσα) and Persephatta (Περσεφάττα). In Latin her name is rendered Proserpina. She was identified by the Romans as the Italic goddess Libera. as:

Libra

In Greek mythology, Persephone (pǝr-SEF-ǝ-nee; Greek: Περσεφόνη), also called Kore (KOR-ee; Greek: Κόρη; KORNJ, "the maiden"), is the daughter of Zeus and Demeter. She became the queen of the underworld through her abduction by Hades, the god of the underworld. The myth of her abduction represents her function as the personification of vegetation, which shoots forth in spring and withdraws into the earth after harvest; hence, she is also associated with spring as well as the fertility of vegetation. Similar myths appear in the cults of male gods like Attis, Adonis, and Osiris, and in Minoan Crete. In some myths, Persephone is the mother of Zeus' son Dionysus, (or Iacchus, and/or Zagreus, as a result of their identification with Dionysus). Persephone was commonly worshipped along with Demeter. To her alone were dedicated the mysteries celebrated at Athens in the month of Anthesterion. In Classical Greek art, Persephone is portrayed carrying a sheaf of grain. She was mostly represented in the process of being carried off by Hades. Her name has numerous historical variants. These include Persephassa (Περσεφάσσα) and Persephatta (Περσεφάττα). She was identified by the Romans as the Italic goddess Libera.

Jupiter as Marduk,

Venus as Ishtar,

Saturn as Ninurta (Ninib),

Mercury as Nabu (Nebo),

Mars as Nergal.

The movements of the Sun, Moon and five planets were regarded as representing the activity of the five gods.

Ishtar

Ishtar, in Mesopotamian religion, goddess of war and sexual love. Ishtar's primary legacy from the Sumerian tradition is the role of fertility figure. Ishtar cult center was Uruk as early as 4,000 BC. Her influence extend to modern-day Iraq, Kuwait and parts of Syria, Iran, and Turkey including the Akkadian, Babylonian and Assyrian Empires. 3000 BC - 2000 BC. Nineveh is a major religious center for the worship of the goddess Ishtar. The first world's written records are as follows: 2285 BC - 2250 BC Life of Enheduanna, daughter of Sargon of Akkad, Priestess, and world's first author known by name. 2150 BC - 1400 BC the Sumerian Epic of Gilgamesh written on clay tablets. 1900 BC - 1600 BC the poem "Descent of Inanna" is written, ritualized, worshipped. Inanna is Ishtar in Sumerian sources. This powerful Mesopotamian goddess is the first known deity for which we have written evidence. The skill of writing is closely related to this period. Later liturgies of all the religions copy the style and ritual recorded on the stone tablets - the call and response, the alphabet as sacred symbols, music and religious poetry to god / gods.

Jupiter

Jupiter (Latin: Iuppiter) is the king of the gods in Roman mythology. He is known as Zeus θεuς in Greek mythology. The Patron God of Babylon was Marduk, Belus or Belos (Ancient Greek: Βῆλος, Vilos) in classical Greek texts in a Babylonian context refers to the Babylonian god as "Bel Marduk". Both Greek Zeus and Roman God Iovis ['jɔwɪs]) also known as JoVe – note the resemblance with JeHoWe were represented as Jupiter, the Main God. Belos was recognized in Babylonian astrology as the planet Jupiter.

In Serbia, at Gamzigrad, all the sculptures point to Dionysus / Galerius, and Romula, the ideological concept of the tetrarchy, being the alpha and omega. Jupiter is present at Gamzigrad as the supreme god. Ancient Greek Plotinus the founder of Neoplatonism metaphorically identified the Demiurge as the Greek God Zeus θεuς. Same as Dios in Rome. Ancient Babylon creation myths appear as writings in Canaan carved letters.

The oldest cuneiform literature of Babylonians divide the fixed stars into three groups: the stars of Anu, Enlil and Ea. Of the planets five were recognized: Jupiter, Venus, Saturn, Mercury and Mars. These five planets were identified with the gods of the Babylonian pantheon as: Jupiter as Bel-Marduk, Venus as Ishtar, Saturn as Ninurta, Ninib, Mercury as Nabu. Nebo, Mars as Nergal. The movements of the Sun, Moon and five planets were regarded as representing the activity of the five gods.

Moon

Sīn or Suen (Akkadian: 𒂗𒍪 EN.ZU or lord-ess of wisdom) or Nanna was the number 30, in cuneiform: 𒌍𒌋 (10 x 3) the god/goddess of the moon in the Mesopotamian religions of Sumer, Akkad, Assyria and Babylonia. Nanna (the classical Sumerian spelling is DŠEŠ.KI = the technical term for the crescent moon, also refers to the deity, is a Sumerian deity worshiped in Ur (Syria you must have guessed).

Sīn or Suen or Nanna was the god of the moon in the Mesopotamian religions. Selene, or Latin Luna, was the personification of the moon as a goddess. She was worshipped at the new and full moons. Many languages have beautiful words for Moon. It is "Luna" in Italian, Latin and Spanish, "Lune" in French, "Mesec" in Slavic, "Mond" in German. Slavic and Germanic countries have the Moon as the male gender. In Babylon SiN was also of a male gender. In Slavic "SiN" means "Son". Luna commonly refers to: Earth's moon, named "Luna" in Latin; Luna (goddess), the ancient Roman personification of the Moon. The ancient sages respected the wisdom of the Moon and its phases. The ancient Chinese called the Sun Tai Yang, or the Great Yang Luminary. They called the Moon Tai Yin, or the Great Yin Luminary. In Hinduism, the Sun is Shiva, while the Moon is Shakti, God and Goddess. Shiva is consciousness, while Shakti is the Soul in its manifestation on Earth. Sīn or Akkadian: 𒌍 EN.ZU or Nanna (Sumerian: 𒀭𒋾 DŠEŠ.KI) was the god of the moon in the Mesopotamian religions of Sumer, Akkad, Assyria and Babylonia.

Goddess Moon or SiN in Ancient Babylon, Sīn or Suen (Akkadian: 𒌍 EN.ZU or lord-ess of wisdom) or Nanna was the number 30, in cuneiform: 𒌍 (10 x 3) the god/goddess of the moon in the Mesopotamian religions of Sumer, Akkad, Assyria and Babylonia. Nanna (the classical Sumerian spelling is DŠEŠ.KI = the technical term for the crescent moon, also refers to the deity, is a Sumerian deity worshiped in Ur (Syria you must have guessed). Sīn or Suen or Nanna was the god of the moon in the Mesopotamian religions. Selene, or Latin Luna, was the personification of the moon as a goddess. She was worshipped at the new and full moons. Many languages have beautiful words for Moon. It is "Luna" in Italian, Latin and Spanish, "Lune" in French, "Mesec" in Slavic, "Mond" in German. Slavic and Germanic countries have the Moon as the male gender. In Babylon SiN was also of a male gender. In Slavic "SiN" means "Son". Luna commonly refers to: Earth's moon, named "Luna" in Latin; Luna (goddess), the ancient Roman personification of the Moon.

Soul

A soul, Aristotle says, is "the actuality of a body that has life," where life means the capacity for self-sustenance, growth, and reproduction. If one regards a living substance as a composite of matter and form, then the soul is the form of a natural—or, as Aristotle sometimes says, organic—body. Plato said that even after death, the soul exists and is able to think. He believed that as bodies die, the soul is continually reborn (metempsychosis) in subsequent bodies. Steiner, observed that the soul has three manifestations called Sentient Soul, Intellectual and Temper Soul and Consciousness Soul. Jung (1954) "Soul" as the "subtle body" and "breath-soul" means something non-material and finer than mere air. Its essential characteristic is to animate and be animated; it therefore represents the life principle. The ancient Egyptians believed that a soul (k❖/b❖; Egypt. pron. ka/ba) was made up of many parts. According to ancient Egyptian creation myths, the god Atum created the world out of chaos, utilizing his own magic (ḥk). Heka existed before duality had yet come into being. The ḫt (khet), or physical form, had to exist for the soul to have intelligence.

Ancient Egypt, you must have guessed, at the centre of Mediterranean, where some wise sages believed that our souls pulsate with the rhythm of magic - HK was the name given to this magic = H as the frequency of Supreme God that expresses IT-SelF through every single individual soul or Ka. Ka / Ba, our soul, they believed has many parts. One of them is the physical body, the spiritual body, the name identity, the personality, the double, the heart, the shadow, the power, and the ❖ḫ finally, that is the symbol used for the soul of the dead once it has completed the transition through the afterlife. How deep and complex the Theology of our ancients was, and how much we can all learn, exploring its secrets. The sacred secret Y has manifested as one of the 3 within the trinity of sounds (Ya-Ho-Wa). Ya moved in its journey carrying male sounds, in

Ancient China taking on the form of G (YanG) and in Ancient Egypt becoming a variety of sounds, R, D, B, G. D carried "da" as the concept of greatness in Chinese, or "tu" as earth, and within the Theosophy of Ancient Europe at the time, D as Pythagoras Do leading the music scale of sounds.

Spiral

Ancient Maltese, Cyprians, Ancient Egyptians, Slavs 6-3,000 BC used Spiral as a symbol of soul's descend to God.

Sun

Sun and Sun worship. As the name of supreme god of many religions, our ancestors used the sound / name and symbol of Sun. Ra vs. Sha or Da (for Dio) vs Na (of iNaNNa). Within many different traditions, we hear our priests narrating the same story. We find the same symbols combined within the Ancient Chinese MinG that is the merge of Ri for Sun and Yue for Moon, meaning = Bright, or in the Ancient Egyptian creation myth within AmoN Ra. The sacred secret Y has manifested as one of the 3 within the trinity of sounds (Ya-Ho-Wa), the sound D carried "da" as the concept of greatness in Chinese, or "tu" as earth, D as Pythagoras Do leading the music scale of sounds. The sacred secret W manifested as the sacred M or N, K or L, P or Ph or as SH of death, or Č for čakra, or Čovek in Slavic, Č that has represented the snake, or the spiral or the Kundalini Force in Ancient Egypt. With the same vibration as Night, Meditation, MiNoS, Mum, Nirvana, Death, it is the YiN of creation. The eye of Horus itself, our sub consciousness or Karma, looking at us, always with the Goddess Isis as M of the Ancient Chinese, that is the eYe, but also a tree, or a mother or a horse.

Trinity and 4 Elements

It has all started and in its puzzling complexity ends with the worship of God (in Arabic the name for God is Allah) or divine, its omnipresent Cosmic entity, in Taoism known as Tao, materialized through trinity of forces (in Hinduism known as rajas, satwas and tamas) within four elements of Gaia: earth, water, sun, and air. In their wisdom Chinese philosophers and ancient sages, even managed to further refine them dividing the manifestations of earth into wood and metal, exploring the dance of five instead of four elements. Within the western worlds, inside the works of greatest philosophers, mystics and artists we find this wisdom sparkled knowledge. Aristotle Plato Pythagoras Within the scientific observations of different types of atoms at similar energy levels, the states with the similar behavior patterns are called: solid, liquid, gas, and plasma. The Ancient Greek system of Aristotle, a student of Plato attending the Plato's Academy found in 387 BC in Athens, better known as the teacher, advisor, consultant of Alexander the Great who was the first one to travel to Egypt.

What is Your Spirit Animal?

How to identify your animal totem?

For Shamans, each animal has a lesson to teach us and main qualities of animals are captured within their animal spirits that come into contact with us to heal us and inspire us in our spiritual journey. Their special energies can teach us and guide us in our search. Ask your inner being: what is my inner animal, my spirit animal, my totem and allow its qualities to inspire you.

Identify any animal that in any way attracts you. Is there a specific animal that fascinates you more than the rest? Is there an animal that you associate yourself with? Is there a quality that you can relate to? Is there an animal that you meet in your dreams or meditations? This is your spirit animal.

What is your animal spirit?

If you fear an animal, it can become your guide. Shamans believe that if you survive an attack of an animal, then that animal is your spirit guide.

'Find Your Spirit Animal' Meditation

Sit comfortably in a silent place.

The meditation can be done inside your home or within your favourite place in nature. It is very good to meditate near the water: a lake, a water source, or near the sea; or in a cave on a mountain top. If you meditate inside, light a candle, switch off any music, your mobile and phone. The best time for any meditation is sunrise or sunset time: early morning or early evening.

Allow all the thoughts to disappear. As a preparation to any meditation you can do some yoga or walk in nature for around 20-30min. It is also good to meditate just after a jog or tai-chi, or chi-gong exercise you just had.

This meditation should last around 30min. Sit straight, relax and enjoy the silence around you for a few minutes. Do not move, just listen to your own breathing. Follow your breath for around 5-10min. It is a simple and very effective zen exercises: just breath in and out, observing your breath. Following your breath you will allow your mind to become quiet.

After, you have focused for long enough to clear your mind from thoughts, work with a visualization exercise that is used by shamans to connect you with your spirit animal. Within your mind, allow your astral body to 'separate' from your physical body. See yourself rising up, leaving your body and the place that surrounds you, and go into a high sacred mountain space. Imagine that the space is filled with amazing beauty and wonder. This phase of meditation will last around 5-10min.

Once you are within your imagined sacred spot, meet your wise man or woman, the one who knows it all and allow the wise man/woman to invite your spirit animal to come and meet you. Let your subconscious give you the answer to the question: what is my spirit animal. Allow this information to flow un-obstructed by thoughts, prejudices, worries, or pre-conceptions. Allow the animal to meet you eye to eye and feel the connection you have with this spiritual being. Feel love towards the animal, the wise man, the surroundings. Take the gift with gratitude and leave the space returning to your meditation spot.

Spirit Animal BEAR

The bear is strong and fast, yet his strength is not immediately obvious. He hibernates for the winter and his main quality is this ability of contemplation. His strength is hidden and his inner wisdom vast. He also represents confidence. Vikings used to wear bear skins in times of war to appear powerful and fearless. Among Northern American Indians the Bear was considered to be a Wise Teacher. The bear is also associated with shamans, so it symbolizes the inner healing abilities.

Spirit Animal BAT

The bat lives in caves and comes out during the night. It represents our unconsciousness. The bat has an inner awareness so it is capable to understand the darkness of the night, the death and the world of dreams. It is known as the 'Guardian of the Night'.

The Native Americans saw bats as symbols of intuition, dreams and visions. People that have this animal as a totem are sensitive and intuitive.

Spirit Animal BIRDS

Falcon and Snake Ancient Egypt name of Horus in Louvre 2500 BC

The birds represent joy, beauty and strength that can kill snakes. They teach us a quality of wonder. They are a symbol of Consciousness.

They represent a mystical link between heaven and earth. In Feng Shui birds are considered a powerful symbol of new opportunities. Angels have wings and we all often dream to fly as birds. Birds are also symbols of freedom and they serve as messengers from heavens

Spirit Animal BUTTERFLY

The butterfly represents inner journeys and dreams. It is a symbol of transformation moving from egg, to larvae (caterpillar), to an amazing beauty of a butterfly. Dreams and art is its major quality. It might have troubles adjusting to a society norms. In many cultures the butterfly is associated with the soul of a recently dead person. Within the Mystical Christianity soul is symbolised as a butterfly and soul's journey is the one of transformation.

Spirit Animal CAT

Bastet Around 600 BC from Saqqara Egypt The British Museum London

Cat is a guardian of underworld. The cat is sensitive, alert and often

233

elegant. It is a symbol of female powers. The cat knows how to relax and yet stay alert. It teaches us how to enjoy life, be in the moment of Now and act when the time is right. In Ancient Egypt cats were sacred and are associated with the Moon Goddess Baset. The Romans also worshiped the cat as a companion of Diana, the Moon Goddess.

Spirit Animal DEER

The deer is gentle, graceful and innocent. The deer offers a quality of inner gentleness, and the fragile nature of a child. It symbolises intuition and psychic abilities. The deer invites you to find your peace in silence.

Spirit Animal DOLPHIN

This animal represents the water element. The dolphin is emotional, creative, sociable, and playful. It is in tune with the rhythms of nature. It represents a person that loves company, action and thrives on fun. Dolphin is the king of fish. Within the Mystical Christianity the dolphin is a symbol of resurrection. In Greek Mythology dolphins carried the souls of the dead to the Islands of the Blessed.

Spirit Animal DRAGON / SNAKE

Νικόλαος Δαμασκηνός 40 AC Ancient Greece

Goddess with Snakes Crete Kronoss Arthmus 1600 BC

The dragon / Snake represents the Life Force Itself. In Asia it is worshiped as a sacred animal. Chinese dragons symbolize control over water, our subconscious forces. The dragon is a symbol of power, a holder of magic powers. It is a teacher, and a magician.

Spirit Animal EAGLE

The eagle represents a free spirit. It rules over Air element and it is its highest representation. The eagle lives alone, flies high and teaches us to face our day-to-day trivialities with courage and to see the world holistically.

The eagle qualities are freedom, determination, clear vision and it teaches us to live our highest potential through clear intentions and ability to manage thoughts.

In Christianity the eagle represents the Christ himself.

Spirit Animal ELEPHANT

The elephant is large and strong, it represents eternal strength and a capability to overcome any obstacle. A famous God in Asia that has an elephant head is Ganesha, a remover of all obstacles. The elephant is kind and respectful of others. They are symbols of wisdom and good luck.

The elephant has quality of stability, determination and loyalty. It stands for high sensitivity and it is a symbol for social connection.

Spirit Animal FOX

The fox is clever. The fox knows how to hide, and how to hunt even in the very busy human inhabited places. The fox is beautiful and it represents our senses, instincts and alertness.

The Celts believed that the fox is a guide, and that it symbolises wisdom.

The fox teaches us determination, and the power of focused mind.

Spirit Animal HORSE

The horse is elegant, strong, and independent. It symbolises personal power and stability. Within the Greek mythology the horse as a healer. It can be trusted, and relied upon. It is a very good friend. In Feng Shui the horse brings the energy of success, fame, and freedom.

The horse brings the balance between instincts and reason. In dreams horses symbolise sexual energy.

For Jung horses symbolize natural forces that we master in our life. They symbolise the core life drive.

Spirit Animal LION

Ancient Akkadian cylinder seal 2334 BC depicting Inanna resting her foot on the back of a lion

The Sphinx of Naxos, also Sphinx of the Naxians, now in the Archaeological Museum of Delphi is a colossal 2 meter tall marble statue of a sphinx a mythical creature with the head of a woman 650 BC

The Lion represents the fire element. The lion is the king of all animals, it represents leadership. The lion walks like a king, talks like a king and moves like a king. It requires attention. If allowed, it is capable to materialise challenging life projects.

In Ancient Greece lions symbolise guardians of the dead and guardians of shrines and temples. In alchemy the lion symbolises Gold. In Buddhism Buddha sits on the lion symbolising strength and wisdom. In Hinduism, the lion is an embodiment of Vishnu.

Spirit Animal OWL

The owl represents wisdom. The owl symbolises stillness. The owl is a symbol of a wise old man that understands the secrets of nature and does not get disturbed by seasonal changes.

The owl teaches us that there is a spring after every winter, and joy after every period of suffering. In Ancient Greece owl is a symbol of Goddess Athena, symbol of intelligence and wealth.

For Native Americans the owl is the keeper of sacred knowledge. For Aboriginals the owl is the messenger of secrets, and a companion of mystics and medicine men.

Spirit Animal TURTLE

The turtle carries its home with it. It needs safety and protection. Once it has a home, it is a symbol for longevity, health and invisible strength. They teach us that moving slowly might be an advantage in a long run. In mythology, turtle represents the moon, immortality, and fertility. In African fairy tales, turtle represents wisdom. In Asia it symbolizing endurance, strength, and longevity. Tortoise shells were used for deviation.

The Ancient Chinese Constellation has four sacred animals that guide the heavens: the Azure Dragon, representing the east, and the wood element, the Vermilion Bird or Fenix of the south representing the fire element, the Black Tortoise that is the ruler of the north tortoise, representing the water element, and White Tiger that protects the west representing metal.

Spirit Animal WOLF

Pharaoh Tutankhamuns tomb, 18th dynasty South Wall

The wolf lives alone. It is independent and it represents a teacher. It materialises projects alone. It has no fears and It takes wisdom from the earth. It is a devoted friend and it knows how to protect its closest.

Spirit Animal BULL

300 BC Ancient Egypt statue Bull Head

Tree Magic

Trees were respected since the beginning of time. Different cultures acknowledged the magic powers within ancient trees and performed various rituals around them. A tree can simply bewitch you offering a sense of mystery and magic, taking you into the journey of green respect towards this witness of time passing, into the wisdom of its mature being. Its roots lie deep in the ground. The leaves draw energy from the sunlight. The trunk is strong and wide. What is the tree hiding: ancient secrets, ghosts, goblins, spirits, ferries or just squirrels?

Druids were priests of an ancient Celtic religious order. They thought that the oak tree is sacred and they carried out their religious rituals in oak forests. They chose the deepest parts of woodlands for their most sacred places.

The Pagans used the Yew tree as the focus of their worship. Apparently, the Yew has a particular quality that inspires a feeling of awe.

The Greeks and Romans decorated their dwellings with ivy, taking evergreen plants into their houses acknowledging their magical qualities.

The Christmas tree is a symbol adopted by Christian tradition, referring to the salvation that Jesus brought to the world by his birth.

Ancient Slav Zodiac

According to the Ancient Slav Zodiac we all have our Tree Signs. Find the date of your birth and enjoy the spiritual meaning of the Tree that protects you. Or learn about the tree that attracts you, it could be your sacred tree.

Oak Tree: 21 March

An Oak Tree is respected as a sacred tree amongst many cultures. Our ancestors used to take important decisions meditating under an oak tree.

If you are born under the protection of this tree you are born to be a leader, a protector, and a guide. You look and act mighty-full and the energy that is given to you is full of creative power. You give an impression of an individual that has a lot of strength. You stay strong and healthy even in your old age. You are brave and carry an ability to change the world. Free and independent with the pure motives you usually work on higher goals and ideals. Followed by the Lady Luck you will flourish if you take care of your 'roots'. The most treasured quality is independence. The worst enemy is. Your openness is contagious, however you might have a difficulty committing to one partner.

Hazelnut tree 22 - 30 March & 24 September - 03 October

A magic fruit tree. Bearing the most delicious edible nuts. A lot of energy follows the people born under the protection of the hazelnut tree. Following your plans to the execution, your initiative often 'feels' like Magic to the others. Your charisma could make you a good leader. The biggest strength is your constant drive to improve and an ability to change your position, home, surroundings. Not afraid of change, and intelligent, you are almost capable of reading other people's thoughts. The biggest weakness could be your intolerance towards the mediocracy. You do not copy others, you are original in your thoughts but also unpredictable. That could cause problems when working with others. Capable of passionate love you could also passionately hate.

A Mountain Ash or Rowan: 01 - 10 April and 04 - 13 October

A Mountain Ash or Rowan is a flowering tree that has pinnate leaves and large clusters of whitish flowers, followed by scarlet berries.

This is a tree of deep feelings. You are capable of deep love, and you expect the same from your partner. You believe in the family and if you settle with the right partner, you will manage to gain the emotional stability. The family base will give or take away your stability. You need to feel secure and you are attracted towards luxury. Usually you will gain the material stability you so desire. Your biggest weakness could be your constant wish to be liked and loved by others.

Acer or Plane Tree: 11 - 20 April and 14 - 23 October

A favourite of the Greeks and Romans; the American sycamore or Eurasian maple tree. In Africa they are thick-branched wide-spreading trees with branches rising from near the ground.

The Acer is the tree of intelligence. People born under the protection of Acer are unusually intelligent. Exploration, new discoveries, and plenty of new ideas always surrounds you. Often ahead of your time, often misunderstood, others find it difficult to follow you.

When young very shy or extravagant, yet always in search for new knowledge, new information, new discoveries. Most often you have success in life, and you enjoy 'bathing' within this success. Attractive to the opposite sex, you find it difficult to appreciate the family life or settle with one partner.

Walnut tree: 21 - 30 April & 24 - 31 October

A Walnut tree needs time and space to mature. The youth that is under the protection of this tree is often shy and insecure, over-emotional and gentle. Yet, with the proper nurturing and care the walnut tree offers the most amazing fruits. Seemingly slow in your action you are very strong and persistent. You always get to your goal. There is no unfinished business within your relationship with others. Your beliefs are strong and you do not compromise. Your feelings are deep and that makes you an honest and devoted friend.

Poplar Tree: 1-14 May; 5 - 13 August; 1-8 Nov & 4-8 February

Poplar has soft light-coloured nondurable wood. It is widely cultivated in the United States and has white bark and leaves with whitish under-surfaces. If you are born under the protection of Poplar you are detailed, precise, and intelligent. In everything you do you execute precision. Freedom is the only God you worship. If you stay honest and truthful you will not need to complicate your relationships with friends, family, or your partner. You are surrounded by influential people and often find yourself in influential positions. Often your family becomes your source of strength and the place where you rest between two 'successes'.

Chestnut tree: 15 - 24 May & 08 - 21 November

A chestnut tree produces edible nuts inside husks. The chestnut tree is a tree of 'rightfulness'. Connected to the rightful doing, thinking and feeling you find any injustice offensive. No matter how many enemies you might create you speak your truth openly. Impulsive and sensitive, you might feel disappointed with the injustice and lies amongst people. This might grow to become a cynicism or emotional coldness. You need the time of silence to withdraw from the world of desires, to re-charge and give yourself a space for the creative impulses.

Ash belonging to the Olive Family: 25 - 03 June & 22 Nov - 01 Dec

An Ash tree is a tree of ambition. Beauty, and the wish to succeed surround you. Your intuition is in sink with your intelligence. You have an ability to deeply understand people, relationships, life. This is a gift that almost feels like 'magic' to others. You often intuitively know the flow of life and its endings. You will succeed in your plans and enjoy your successes. Your work might become famous during your life-time or after your death.

Sour Cherry Tree: 04 - 13 June and 02 - 11 December

A sour cherry tree is the tree of art. You are deeply moved by beauty and all its manifestations so you seek it all around you. A sportsman, or a special diet-follower you will work on your vitality and health until the old age. You look for beauty in all. If you are surrounded with beauty your energy will flourish.

Fig Tree: 14 - 20 June and 12 - 21 December

A Fig Tree is a tree of feelings. The olives absorb the energy around them. The olive oil has to be kept closely tight in a small container because it will absorb the scents of the surroundings. You are capable to understand the whole spectrum of feelings. Good natured, gentle and sentimental your happiness is not stable. The other people's un-friendliness deeply hurt you and their friendliness make you happy. In an attempt to please others, sometimes you are too strict towards yourself or your children. You are a faithful partner and that makes you very attractive to the opposite sex. You appreciate the values of the family and you will work hard to establish their happiness. It is the family that gives you security and you need their constant appreciation. Your work is slow but consistent and with your persistency you will achieve results. You find it difficult to start your projects but once you start them you will finalise them. Often you get sick during the cold winters.

Birch: 21. June

If you are born during the longest day in the year you are beautiful, elegant and refined. You are energetic and your optimism is contagious. Friendly you are good natured and charming. You could be a writer, or a leader because you are not afraid of big projects. You could do a lot for the benefit of others. Your good looks, creativity and charisma open the door to your endeavours. You do not forget your life lessons and your memory is great. In love you follow both intuition and intelligence and work to have a passionate relationship even with your long-term partner. You have a quality of a Divine Madman but you do appreciate your family and home.

Beech 22. December

A Beech is a tree of beauty. Beauty and dignity is your middle name. You keep your good looks until your old age. To stay beautiful is a must so you work on your fitness, diets, or even go for a plastic surgery to stop the aging process. You follow fashion and like good clothes. In youth you might be mis-understood and unhappy often because of the unhappy love. Later in life you prove to be a faithful partner searching one deep love affair. You should look for a partner that is an optimist to bring some laughter into your life. If you are disappointed in love, you could easily turn towards hate. When you hit your mid-life crises, you might be the one to wish to change the partner, seeking eternal youth. Your best moments are later on in life when your organising abilities come into full force. You will have money.

Apple Tree: 22. June - 04. July and 23. December - 01 January

People under the protection of an apple tree are extraordinary gifted. Many cultured considered the apple tree to be the tree of love. You are beautiful, attractive and you constantly think about love. For you falling in love happens every day and you enjoy the ecstasy of love-making. The love can be 'secret', 'passionate', 'jealous' and since you are thirsty for love you might experience them all. Stay honest and open within your relationship so not to complicate them too much. For you it is difficult to stay faithful. You earn and spend your money easily cause you are not attached to it so often you find yourself in debt. You live in the moment of Now, and that could make you a victim of not-real friends.

A Fir Tree: 05. - 14. July and 02 - 11. January

A Fir tree is a tree of mysticism and the people born under the protection of this tree are surrounded by art, mysticism, music. Women like to wear jewellery, and men get attracted to antiques. You have a stable health and a long life. The danger is that you could become an egoist that appreciate his or her collection more than people. It is very good for you to have children and live in a family life returning back to the true life values. Aware of your weaknesses you try to transform them into virtues. Very intelligent, completely conscientious and very persistent you can overtake any obstacle. You have strong willpower and you are very patient. If you turn towards the 'love training' you will open your heart and start appreciate your partner more.

Elm: 15. - 25. July and 12. - 24. January

An elm is a tree of attractiveness. If you are born under the protection of this tree you will be very attractive, you also have a strong sense of justice giving hard time to both yourself and others. Open and honest, you are a faithful friend. You take care of your health until your old age. Peaceful and relaxed you do care for others, especially your family members. You are patient with kids and could be very gentle with animals. Your love life is very rich and you fight for your ideal all throughout your life. Because of your stability, optimism and nationalism, you might become a politician. The family harmony, the long-term relationships with your partner and friends, the secure home environment are all very important for your emotional security. Your weakness might be your sense of security vs. your wish to expand into new horizons. Nurture your creativity and focus your intention and you will succeed.

Cypress Tree: 26. July - 04. August and 25. January - 03. February

A Cypress tree is a tree of faithfulness in love, in business and in friendship. Truly a monogamous creature, both men and women find their love within one partner. Capable to adapt to all situations you are satisfied with the little, you believe that the happiness is not within the possessions but within the lack of desires. Honour is your strongest virtue. You can trust your-own ability to succeed in life that is why you usually do your chore on your-own. You have to learn to trust other people abilities and delegate your work so that you get that extra help and live into your old age.

Almond Tree 14. - 23. August and 09. - 18. February

An almond tree is a tree native to Asia and North Africa having the prettiest pink blossoms and highly prized edible nuts.

The almond is the tree of optimism. If you are born under the influence of this tree you can adapt to all situations and become a very good manager. Your self-confidence is contagious, your charisma takes you into many love relationships and good business deals. You love the love and life game and falling in love is a part of your life rhythm. Open, giving, friendly you enjoy art, music and sports. You appreciate money as a tool for your entertainment. You are a self-centred perfectionist and that can also be your major weakness.

Pine Tree: 24. August - 02. September and 19. - 29. February

A Pine Tree is a tree of refinement. The pine gives people born under its influence a gentle, refine body that love to be surrounded with beauty and luxury. You cannot stand ignorance, vulgar behaviour and dirt. You know what you want and how to get to where you want. No defeats can harm you and your goal is always ahead. Intelligent and precise, you can become a millionaire. Be aware not to close your heart. Your weakness is within your ego-centric nature and your lack of compromise.

Willow: 03. - 12. September and 01. - 10. March

A Willow is a tree of Sensibility. Our ancestors thought that ghosts dance under the willow trees. Sensual and with a strong interest for spiritual life your intuition coupled with your perception makes you a natural medium. Your 6th sense is strong and gives you a balanced philosophical attitude toward life. You are sensitive and gentle needing of lot of care and love. A happy family structure is a must so that you can flourish. You are a dreamer, a nature-lover, a romantic, sometimes a melancholic. You are an artist with an amazing inner strength that has no exhibitions unless s/he truly relies on the inborn self-confidence and a world-traveller that dreams of home. You are an unfaithful lover who believes in love, its strength and romance. You prefer to rely on your intuition that on your mind.

Linden tree: 13 - 22. September and 11 - 20. March

A Linden tree is a tree with heart-shaped leaves and drooping cymose clusters of yellowish often fragrant flowers. It is a tree of wizards. Born under the protection of this tree you are deeply connected to secret societies, occult happenings and magic. Beautiful as youth you become over-weight in the old age. With your practical intelligence you are organised, clean and precise and you demand this from your family. If your focus is within the 'purity' of the spiritual work you will find your soul-mate and nurture a happy family. Your strong intuition over-powers your sense of the practical analysis. Finding the balance between the two is your key to happiness.

Cherry Tree: 23. September

People born under the protection of the cherry tree are unhappy whenever there is no sun. Aware of it you often try to move to tropical places to combat the rheumatism. Peaceful, tolerant and wise you do not like violence. Live as you please and let others live is your moto. The only time you get really mad is when someone betrays you. The betrayals can take the worst of you. Friendly, you are loved by many, your laughter is loud and contagious, as though you spread sun around you. The centre of attention your magnetism is obvious. You do not understand envy and jealousy. You have a philosophical attitude towards life, its successes and failures. It is a pleasure to be around you.

ABOUT THE AUTHOR

Nataša Pantović is Serbian Maltese Novelist, Management Consultant, Adoptive Parent and Ancient Worlds Researcher that lives in Malta.
Author of 9 AoL Mindfulness Books.
Published Authro since 1991.

After helping Father George build a school in a remote area of Ethiopia, Nataša entered the most amazing world of parenting adopting kids from Ethiopia as a single mum.
Nataša says that her kids are her biggest Conscious Parenting Teachers.

Nataša has traveled through more than 50 countries and lived in 5: UK, New Zealand, Holland, Serbia and Malta. Worked in KPMG, Delloite, Reeds Consulting, in Malta and the Uk as Head of Business Development, Management Trainer, International Speaker. As a Volonteer she has organised various Body Mind Spirit Festivals in Malta, International Veggetarina Festival, Metgeum Conference. She now writes and lectures about variety of applied psychology and self-development topics.

Spiritual Symbols with their Meanings
© Artof4Elements / Februar 14 2018

ISBN 978-9995754129

Pantović Nataša, Spiritual Symbols
-English-

Published by Artof4Elements
4, Holly Wood, St. Albert Street, Gzira GZR1157,
Malta

www.artof4elements.com

Made in the USA
Monee, IL
21 October 2022

16318981R00144